God's DAILY ANSWER

365 devotions — one for each day of the year.

devotions to renew your soul

Do you have questions about God? If so, you're not alone. Most people regularly ponder the mysteries of God. Many questions will not be answered until we meet Him face-to-face in eternity. The answers are too weighty for the human mind to grasp. But there is much we can and do know about God because He's chosen to explain Himself—primarily through the Scriptures.

God's Daily Answer Devotional was created to give you a daily dose of God's revealed truth, answer some of the questions that can be answered, and give you the assurance that God wants you to know Him. As you read through the scripture, meditation, and quote for each day, ask God to help you take hold of the answer contained therein and establish it in your heart. Record your thoughts in the space given for daily reflection. Doing so will help you gain ownership of what you have just learned. We hope you will then be well on your way to a lifetime of discovering God.

Love is kind.

1 CORINTHIANS 13:4 NRSV

The dictionary defines "kindness" as an attribute of someone who is gentle, generous, friendly, and benevolent. What a beautiful picture of how God extends Himself. And what a great example for you as you reach out to those around you.

Kindness is more than an attitude; it's an action. It looks for ways to meet needs and make others smile. Pause for a moment and think about all the ways God has been kind to you. Then, ask Him to help you extend yourself in kindness to those whose lives you touch—including the strangers who move through your life each day. Your actions may be just the answer to prayer someone needs.

A kind heart is a fountain of gladness,
making everything in its vicinity freshen into smiles.

WASHINGTON IRVING

YOUR DAILY REFLECTIONS

_____

_____

_____

_____

*Grow in the grace and knowledge of our Lord
and Savior Jesus Christ.*

2 PETER 3:18 NCV

When you plant a seed, you don't expect it to blossom into a beautiful flower by dawn the next morning. Growth takes time and nourishment. The same is true for the seed God has planted in you.

You have everything you need to bloom—the light of God's presence, the water of His Word, and the soil of His grace. Together these create the perfect garden environment for a thriving plant like you. But you also need time.

Don't despair when you find yourself caught in winter's chilly grip. Growth is still taking place. It's just harder to see. So be patient with yourself. Promise of a fruitful spring is right around the corner.

Be not afraid of growing slowly;
be afraid only of standing still.

CHINESE PROVERB

YOUR DAILY REFLECTIONS

_____

_____

_____

_____

You are my hiding place. You protect me from my troubles.
PSALM 32:7 NCV

Children find comfort in hiding places. Whether it's the privacy of a tree fort or a cubby hole under the sink, there's a sense of security that comes from being protected on all sides.

Grown-ups still seek hiding places. They may no longer hide in the closet, but many of them choose to hide in their work, in relationships, or even in what they find in the fridge. These places may offer temporary comfort, but they cannot offer protection. Only God can do that.

Whatever troubles you may be facing, whatever fear has taken hold of your heart, you can run to God anytime. He is your ultimate hiding place, surrounding you with the protective love only the Father can have for His beloved child.

Security is not the absence of danger,
but the presence of God, no matter what the danger.
AUTHOR UNKNOWN

YOUR DAILY REFLECTIONS

_____

_____

_____

_____

See if I will not open the windows of heaven
for you and pour down for you an overflowing blessing.

MALACHI 3:10 NRSV

God is a giver. He doesn't wait for birthdays or special occasions. He wraps each new day in a sunrise and presents it to you with open arms. He's prepared not just one perfect gift, but more blessings than you can count. The first breath you take when you awake, a cup of coffee to sip, a hand to hold, a memory that makes you smile ... every single moment of your life is filled with more blessings than your human mind can possibly comprehend.

But, that doesn't mean you shouldn't try. Take a moment right now. Ask God to make you aware of the blessings He is bringing your way today. Bask in His goodness. Then, offer Him a thank-you note of praise.

The best things are nearest; breath in your nostrils,
light in your eyes, flowers at your feet,
duties at your hand, the path of God just before you.

ROBERT LOUIS STEVENSON

YOUR DAILY REFLECTIONS

_____

_____

_____

_____

Choose life that both you and your descendants may live.
DEUTERONOMY 30:19

Some choices are easy ... Paper or plastic? Regular or unleaded? For here or to go? Others take a lot more wisdom: Which job should I take? Where should I live? Whom should I marry? How can I be a better parent? What is a wise use of my finances?

Every day is filled with choices, both big and small. And God wants to help you make them wisely. He's already given you what you need: the wisdom and understanding included in the Bible—through precept and example—God's whisper in your heart, and the acquired wisdom of family and friends.

Make those easy choices yourself, but when you need some help with tough decisions, God is ready and willing to point you down the right path.

God always gives his very best to those
who leave the choice with him.
JAMES HUDSON TAYLOR

YOUR DAILY REFLECTIONS

_____

_____

_____

_____

Humble yourselves before the Lord, and he will lift you up.
JAMES 4:10 NIV

You are God's priceless treasure—unique in beauty, design, and potential. There are accomplishments and victories you have achieved that you can be proud of. God is certainly proud of the person you've become. But, if you look closely, you almost certainly will have to admit that everything you are and everything you've done can be traced back to God.

That's why humility is more than a positive character trait—it's a paradox. It's holding in one hand how much you've achieved and in the other how deeply dependent you are on the One who has helped you achieve it. So, when you receive praise from others, pause for a moment to put everything into perspective and humble yourself before the Lord.

Humility is nothing else but a true knowledge
and awareness of oneself as one really is.
THE CLOUD OF UNKNOWING

YOUR DAILY REFLECTIONS

_____

_____

_____

_____

> *My dear friends, you should be quick to listen*
> *and slow to speak.*
>
> JAMES 1:19 CEV

There is no such thing as idle chitchat. Every one of your words has power. When you string them together with forethought and grace, they can diffuse an argument, teach a friend a new skill, or soothe the heart of a disappointed child. But, on occasion, words can slip through your lips that you wish you could take back.

God wants to help slow you down. Like a car, your tongue is easier to control at slower speeds. That's why learning to listen is an important part of speaking with love. Listening to people's hearts, as well as their words, will help you stop long enough to gather your thoughts. Then choose your words carefully, so you can use them in a powerful, positive way.

It is easier to look wise than to talk wisely.

SAINT AMBROSE

YOUR DAILY REFLECTIONS

_____

_____

_____

_____

The LORD said, "I have loved you with an everlasting love."
                                                    JEREMIAH 31:3 NIV

I f love came with a lifetime guarantee, it would be easier to give and receive. You could risk sharing your heart fully with another. You would never fear rejection. You could trust that the words and actions of anyone who loved you would always be in your best interest.

There is only one love that comes with such a guarantee—and that love lasts even longer than your lifetime. That's the love of God. Knowing that God's love for you is unshakeable gives you the confidence to be yourself. You are wholly accepted, fully forgiven, and eternally loved. What response does thinking about that truth evoke in your heart?

The person you are now, the person you have been,
            the person you will be—this person
                  God has chosen as beloved.
                                        WILLIAM COUNTRYMAN

YOUR DAILY REFLECTIONS

_____

_____

_____

_____

In all the work you are doing, work the best you can.
Work as if you were working for the Lord, not for men.

COLOSSIANS 3:23 NCV

There is a sense of accomplishment in a job well done, whether it's raising a child, finishing a business proposal, or mowing the lawn. But, there are plenty of days when work feels more like drudgery. Sometimes, the only thing that keeps you going is knowing you have bills to pay and a long list of chores that need to be done.

But, that's not the whole story. Every job you do is a gift you present to your heavenly Father. The excellence you put into each task reflects how beautiful you want that gift to be. So, whatever work you have before you today, put your whole heart into it—and picture God watching you proudly from the sidelines.

Work is not a curse, it is a blessing from God.

JOHN PAUL II

YOUR DAILY REFLECTIONS

_____

_____

_____

_____

My soul, wait silently for God alone,
for my expectation is from Him.

PSALM 62:5

When parents are awaiting the arrival of a baby, we say they are "expecting." This time of expectation affects every aspect of their lives. Whether the days are easy or rough, what lies ahead makes it all worth it. The sense of expectation grows along with the precious child inside its mother.

Even if you are not "expecting" a child, you should still live an expectant life. God has great things ahead for you. Some may take place slowly throughout your lifetime, while others will catch you in a moment of joyous surprise. Expect God to do good things in your life. Wait for them, anticipate them, prepare for them. Keep your eyes open. Adventure awaits.

High expectations are the key to everything.

SAM WALTON

YOUR DAILY REFLECTIONS

_____

_____

_____

_____

He counts the number of the stars; He calls them all by name.
PSALM 147:4

Children, pets, even cars—people name what's important to them. So does God. God's glorious creation of nature is more than just an arts-and-crafts project completed by an almighty hand. The Bible says that God is evident in everything He has created. In other words, you can get a sense of God's greatness whenever you take a walk in the woods, work in the yard, or gaze out over the ocean.

Spend some time getting to know God's handiwork a little better. Ponder the intricacy of a wildflower. Watch the miracle of a butterfly in flight. Look up at the stars and remember—God has named each one, but you mean more to Him than the entire Milky Way.

The more I study nature,
the more I am amazed at the Creator.
LOUIS PASTEUR

YOUR DAILY REFLECTIONS

_____

_____

_____

_____

Jesus said, "Greater love has no one than this,
than to lay down one's life for his friends.
You are My friends if you do whatever I command you."

JOHN 15:13–14

One way God puts His arms around you is through your circle of friends. Whom has He brought into your life? Picture their faces. Think of the ways God has shown His love to you through them. Then, do something to show that you love them in return. Pray for them.

You can support your friends in many ways. You can join them in celebrating their victories, walk beside them when they need moral support, and just share a laugh to brighten up the day. But, taking time to ask God to care for them, in ways only He can, is a true sign of friendship.

Friendship is one of the sweetest joys of life.
Many might have failed beneath the bitterness
of their trial had they not found a friend.

CHARLES HADDON SPURGEON

YOUR DAILY REFLECTIONS

_____

_____

_____

_____

I will sing of your love and justice;
to you, O LORD, I will sing praise.

PSALM 101:1 NIV

Justice is cause for joy. For those who are innocent, it is a welcome promise to set things right. For those who are guilty, it is a time of reckoning. Knowing that God is just is also a constant reassurance that He will not change the rules of life as you go along. Right will always be right and wrong will always be wrong.

Consider what life would be like if God were not just. He would be unpredictable. He could be cruel one minute, then apathetic the next. An all-powerful God who is not just would be someone to be feared, not loved.

Knowing that God is just means you can relax. Once you've asked for His forgiveness, you have it.

Justice and power must be brought together,
so that whatever is just may be powerful,
and whatever is powerful may be just.

BLAISE PASCAL

YOUR DAILY REFLECTIONS

_____

_____

_____

_____

This is what the Lord says:…
I will comfort you as a mother comforts her child.

ISAIAH 66:12–13 NCV

Being a parent is a tough job, but a rewarding one. It takes a balance of discipline and delight, confrontation and comfort, holding on and letting go. God is familiar with both the joys and the challenges of parenthood. He revels in raising you.

Recognizing that you are as dependent on your heavenly Father as a young child is on his or her parents can help you keep life in perspective. It can also make you wiser with your own children. When confronting a challenge, ask yourself, "How would God be a loving Father to me in this situation?" Then, show the same wisdom and compassion to the children God has placed in your life.

Be the soul support of your children.

AUTHOR UNKNOWN

YOUR DAILY REFLECTIONS

_____

_____

_____

_____

May my meditation be sweet to Him.

PSALM 104:34

When you're trying to solve a problem, you turn it over in your mind, looking at it from every angle. You ruminate, contemplate, and meditate on it. Spending time doing the same thing about God can draw you closer to Him. It can also make Him smile.

Meditating on God can be done anytime, anywhere. You can ponder His attributes, His words from the Bible, His creation, and the wonderful things He's done in your life. Set aside time each day just to think about God. Ask Him to reveal Himself more clearly to you. Look at what you know about Him from every angle. Consider how to apply what you discover. And remember—not a moment goes by that God's not thinking about you.

In the rush and noise of life, as you have intervals,
step home within yourselves and be still. Wait upon God,
and feel his good presence; this will carry you
evenly through your day's business.

WILLIAM PENN

YOUR DAILY REFLECTIONS

_____

_____

_____

Blessed is the man who keeps on going when times are hard.
JAMES 1:12 NIrV

Learning to walk takes perseverance. Just watch any toddler-in-training. The victory of making it across the room on wobbly legs comes only after repeated face-plants into the carpet. But, children don't give up. As they look up at the faces of their proud parents, they are inspired to keep trying until they succeed.

God knows there are times in your life that are much more difficult than learning how to walk. But, He's there, like any loving parent, supporting you if you start to take a tumble. When you feel discouraged and thoughts of quitting begin to run through your head, look up. Your proud Father is close by with His arms open wide, encouraging you to move forward, one step at a time.

Permanence, perseverance, and persistence in spite of
all obstacles, discouragements, and impossibilities:
It is this that in all things distinguishes
the strong soul from the weak.
SIR FRANCIS DRAKE

YOUR DAILY REFLECTIONS

Be doers of the word, and not hearers only.

JAMES 1:22

The Bible is a good book. It contains exciting history, challenging prophecy, and sound advice. You could read it just like any other time-honored classic and walk away inspired. But, the Bible offers you something better— the chance to walk away changed.

That's because the Bible is different from other good books you may have on your shelf. It is the actual Word of God. As you read, God's Spirit whispers to your heart how this ancient text directly applies to your life today. Throughout the Old and New Testaments, God will guide you, challenge you, and comfort you. The only loving response to this love letter from your heavenly Father is to act on what you've read.

God did not write a book and send it by messenger
to be read at a distance by unaided minds.
He spoke a Book and lives in His spoken words,
constantly speaking His words and causing
the power of them to persist across the years.

A. W. TOZER

YOUR DAILY REFLECTIONS

_____

_____

_____

The joy of the Lord will make you strong.

NEHEMIAH 8:10 NCV

When your heart is full of joy, it spills over into every other area of your life. It makes hard tasks appear easier, aggravating situations seem less annoying, and disappointment feel less devastating. In short, it gives you the strength to face tough times. And it just makes life more fun.

Joy goes deeper than circumstance. It isn't dependent upon you winning the lottery or even being able to squeeze in your favorite activity. True joy, the kind that doesn't disappear when times get hard, is dependent on one thing—God's presence in your life. Knowing God is near and that He promises to bring good out of every circumstance in your life is a source of joy that will never run dry.

Happiness depends on what happens; joy does not.

OSWALD CHAMBER

YOUR DAILY REFLECTIONS

_____

_____

_____

_____

*Jesus said to them, "Take care! Be on your guard
against all kinds of greed; for one's life does not consist
in the abundance of possessions."*

LUKE 12:5 NRSV

Money is an important tool. It helps you feed and clothe your family, as well as afford a night out every now and then. But, it's just a tool. Falling in love with it would be as foolish as becoming infatuated with your lawn furniture.

Keeping your spending under control is a sign that you and money have an appropriate relationship. Your budget shows where your true priorities lie. If a large portion of your monthly income is spent entertaining yourself or purchasing wants instead of needs, it's time to ask God—and perhaps a financial planner—for help. Using your finances wisely not only honors God, it also encourages you to keep your eyes on those things that really matter.

Use everything as if it belongs to God. It does.
You are his steward.

AUTHOR UNKNOWN

YOUR DAILY REFLECTIONS

_____

_____

_____

_____

Don't copy the behavior and customs of this world,
but let God transform you into a new person
by changing the way you think.

ROMANS 12:2 NLT

Optimists and pessimists can look at the same circumstances and see two totally different scenarios. The only real difference is in their minds. The way people think helps determine the way they act. The way people act reflects what they believe to be true.

God wants to change your mind, literally. He wants to change worry to prayer, fear to trust, and doubt to faith. To do that, you need to choose which thoughts you're going to focus on. Reflect on what God says is true about you and the world. Reject what you see on TV or read in a magazine that conflicts with that truth. Filling your mind with good, positive things will result in a good, positive outlook on life.

Change your thoughts and you change your world.

NORMAN VINCENT PEALE

YOUR DAILY REFLECTIONS

_____

_____

_____

_____

The Lord will keep his promises.
With love he takes care of all he has made.

PSALM 145:13 NCV

Think about just a few of the promises God has given you. He's promised to love you, forgive you, fight for you, comfort you, answer your prayers according to His plan, and spend eternity with you, to name just a few.

God has never made a promise that He could not or would not keep. That means you can trust Him with your deepest secrets, biggest dreams, and greatest fears. You can take Him at His Word and move forward in the direction He's asked you to go—with total confidence.

Even when it's difficult to see God at work in your circumstances, His faithfulness is your assurance that He's not only active and involved, but He's using the situation to bring good into your life.

In God's faithfulness lies eternal security.

CORRIE TEN BOOM

YOUR DAILY REFLECTIONS

_____

_____

_____

_____

All of you be of one mind, having compassion for one another.
1 PETER 3:8

Putting yourself in someone else's shoes isn't a fashion opportunity. It's called empathy. Whether you're watching the news, talking to a friend, or taking special note of a stranger, imagine what life would be like if you traded places. Putting yourself in another's shoes will help open your eyes to the needs around you. Then you're ready to move from empathy to compassion—which is merely empathy in action.

Ask God to reveal which needs are ones that you can help fill. That may be helping a friend with a project, offering a much-needed hug, or simply saying a prayer. No matter how you reach out to others, compassion is another way of letting God's love flow through your life into the lives of others.

By compassion we make others' misery our own,
and so, by relieving them, we relieve ourselves also.
SIR THOMAS BROWNE

YOUR DAILY REFLECTIONS

_____

_____

_____

_____

*Jesus said, "Where two or three are gathered together
in My name, I am there in the midst of them."*

MATTHEW 18:20

When birds migrate south for the winter, they do not make the journey alone. They fly together, supporting one another in formation. They take turns leading, flying first into the wind. They work as a team for protection, efficiency, and companionship.

The Church is God's design for His flock. It is how God's children support one another along their journey of life. While learning more about God's Word on Sunday mornings is part of being involved in a local church, it's just the beginning. Dare to reach out. Get involved. Build relationships. Join a Bible study group. Use your unique talents to serve others. Be open to letting others serve you when you are in need. Spread your spiritual wings and soar.

The church is not wood and stone,
but the company of people who believe in Christ.

MARTIN LUTHER

YOUR DAILY REFLECTIONS

_____

_____

_____

_____

May he give you the desire of your heart
and make all your plans succeed.

PSALM 20:4 NIV

The word "success" brings to mind a prestigious job, a hefty bank account, or a home in an upscale neighborhood. In God's eyes, however, success paints a very different picture … a parent who raises a godly child, a friend who overcomes betrayal with forgiveness, a person who simply steps out in courage to be exactly who God has created him or her to be.

True success is honoring God in whatever you do. On occasion, those around you may regard your efforts as a failure, but that doesn't mean Heaven isn't cheering.

Put your plans in God's hands. Do your best. Then, thank God for all He helps you achieve. In God's eyes, that's how every person can dress for success.

I have only to be true to the highest I know—
success or failure is in the hands of God.

E. STANLEY JONES

YOUR DAILY REFLECTIONS

_____

_____

_____

_____

The LORD said, "My Presence will go with you,
and I will give you rest."

EXODUS 33:14

Look at your "To-Do" list for the day. Chances are there is something you've forgotten to write down. Don't panic. It's not another obligation. It's simple relaxation.

God does not just care about what you *do*. He cares about you. He knows your body gets tired, and you need to stop regularly to rest. Taking a break from life's demands by getting a good night's sleep, reading a book, taking a walk, or enjoying a vacation is not self-indulgent. It's a gift from God to you.

When life starts to weigh heavily on your shoulders or your heart, stop—even if just for a moment. Picture yourself in Jesus' arms. Relax. He loves you—even when your "To-Do" list isn't finished.

Take rest; a field that has rested gives a bountiful crop.

OVID

YOUR DAILY REFLECTIONS

_____

_____

_____

_____

*There is now no condemnation for those who are in
Christ Jesus, because through Christ Jesus the law of
the Spirit of life set me free from the law of sin and death.*

ROMANS 8:1–2 NIV

If you break your favorite vase, no amount of glue can return it to its original beauty. The cracks will always show. Choosing your own way over God's breaks your relationship with Him. But, God offers something that will not only mend this relationship, but make it as good as new—His forgiveness.

All you need to do to receive God's forgiveness is ask for it. It sounds easy, but acknowledging your deep need for God means putting aside your pride. It means getting down on your knees physically or mentally and reaching up to the One who is reaching down to you. Take time to do that now. Do it as often as you need to. God's forgiveness knows no end.

There is only one person God cannot forgive:
the one who refuses to come to him for forgiveness.

AUTHOR UNKNOWN

YOUR DAILY REFLECTIONS

_____

_____

_____

_____

Share with God's people who are in need. Practice hospitality.
ROMANS 12:13 NIV

Practicing hospitality may be simpler than you think. It doesn't require that you have a fancy home, wear a chef's hat, or develop a flair for entertaining. All it takes is love. When you open your heart to others, opening your home comes naturally—even when there are chores to do, the kids are wrestling in the family room, and you're exhausted from a long day at work.

The goal of hospitality is to make others feel comfortable. That means spending time getting to know your guests, rather than just serving their physical needs. It means welcoming both friends and acquaintances, anticipating that God has brought you together for a purpose. It means opening your heart in unexpected ways to unexpected people.

Hospitality is one form of worship.
JEWISH PROVERB

YOUR DAILY REFLECTIONS

_____

_____

_____

_____

We believe with our hearts,
and so we are made right with God.

ROMANS 10:10 NCV

Kids believe anything you tell them—for example, that they were delivered via stork, a fairy took the teeth that were placed under their pillows, Santa Claus ate the cookies they left by the tree. But, adults want proof before they put their faith in anything.

Consider what your belief in God is based on. Is it the result of growing up in a religious family? Do you think it's just the right thing to do? Do you know why the Bible can be trusted?

God wants your belief in Him to be something you can stake your life on, in this world and for the next. If you have doubts, ask questions. Look for answers in the Bible. Ask God for direction. Then, move forward with confidence in what you believe.

We can believe what we choose.
We are answerable for what we choose to believe.

JOHN HENRY NEWMAN

YOUR DAILY REFLECTIONS

_____

_____

_____

_____

Let your gentleness be known to everyone.

PHILIPPIANS 4:5 NRSV

Like a snowflake that falls silently from the sky, softly coming to rest on a tender branch, a person who exhibits gentleness touches the lives of others. Such a person's loving presence never demands center stage and yet is noticed. A gentle person knows that gentleness is not a symptom of weakness, but a sign of strength. That's because such a person is secure in who God has created him or her to be.

God, though all-powerful, is also gentle. When you choose not to force your plans, opinions, or desires upon others, you imitate Him. When you return a gentle word for a harsh one or offer a tender embrace to a troubled heart, you are showing the world that you are your Father's child.

Power can do by gentleness
what violence fails to accomplish.

LATIN PROVERB

YOUR DAILY REFLECTIONS

_____

_____

_____

_____

If anyone belongs to Christ, then he is made new.
The old things have gone; everything is made new!
All this is from God.

2 CORINTHIANS 5:17–18 NCV

Anything that is brand-new has an appealing quality to it. The first blossoms of spring. The rhythmic breathing of a sleeping puppy. That new-car smell. The silky skin of a newborn baby. The promise of a fresh start.

God is the author of fresh starts and brand-new beginnings. When you choose to follow Him, your life is transformed from the inside out. You are a totally new person, with new priorities, new power, new purpose, and a new eternal destiny.

But, this isn't just a one-time transformation. God gives you a fresh start every time you need one—morning by morning or minute by minute. All you need to do is ask.

With each sunrise, we start anew.

AUTHOR UNKNOWN

YOUR DAILY REFLECTIONS

_____

_____

_____

_____

Do not be interested only in your own life,
but be interested in the lives of others.

PHILIPPIANS 2:4 NCV

Something significant happens when people spend time together. They become committed to one another—providing support during hard times, challenging each other to do what is right, and celebrating each other's victories as if they were their own.

To build a bond of fellowship in your own life, ask God to show you an area in your church or community where you can become more active or a group of people you could get to know on a deeper level. Then, risk sharing your life honestly and openly. Ask for prayer when you need it. Pray regularly for those God brings into your life to support you. Enjoy being there for one another. You weren't meant to spend your life alone.

Be united with other Christians. A wall with loose bricks is not good. The bricks must be cemented together.

CORRIE TEN BOOM

YOUR DAILY REFLECTIONS

_____

_____

_____

_____

*Remember this: Whoever sows sparingly
will also reap sparingly, and whoever sows generously
will also reap generously.*

2 CORINTHIANS 9:6 NIV

A generous person is one who reaches out to those in need. Does that describe you? If so, your willingness to share your time and treasures sends the message that people are valuable. Your actions say, "What is of worth to God is of worth to me."

This kind of other-centered generosity flows naturally from a grateful heart. The more you recognize how much you've been given, the easier it is to share. Consider in what areas God has been exceedingly generous to you, and find ways to practice generosity with what you've been given. Then, go one step further. Ask God to help you be generous even when you feel you have "just enough." God can take a little and turn it into a lot.

You are never more like God than when you give.

AUTHOR UNKNOWN

YOUR DAILY REFLECTIONS

_____

_____

_____

_____

Have courage, and be strong.

1 CORINTHIANS 16:13 NCV

You don't have to be standing on a battlefield to live a life of valor. Every time you move forward in the face of fear, you prove that you're a courageous person. That doesn't mean you never feel afraid. All it means is that you don't let your feelings prevent you from doing what you know God wants you to do.

You know what your personal battlefields are. Perhaps you're holding a firm line of integrity in your job, when it would be easier and more comfortable to let little indiscretions slide. Or maybe you're facing an illness that has left your life in uncertainty. Whatever the battle, step out in courage. God will never let you face those challenges alone.

Courage is fear that has said its prayers.

DOROTHY BERNARD

YOUR DAILY REFLECTIONS

_____

_____

_____

_____

Teach us to number our days,
that we may apply our hearts unto wisdom
PSALM 90:12 KJV

Academic degrees can show that you are knowledgeable, but only a life well lived can show that you are wise. Wisdom isn't something that you gain automatically as you grow older. Often, it's something you acquire by gleaning insights from the company you keep.

Spending time with people who are more mature than you are—in their faith, their marriages, and as parents—is one of wisdom's most pleasant classrooms. When you put what you learn from their words and lives into practice, discernment and good judgment are sure to mature in your own life.

But, no matter how wise your mentors, there's no substitute for spending time with the source of wisdom—God Himself. He promises wisdom to anyone who asks.

The next best thing to being wise oneself
is to live in a circle of those who are.
C. S. LEWIS

YOUR DAILY REFLECTIONS

_____

_____

_____

_____

Lord, tell me your ways. Show me how to live.
Guide me in your truth.

PSALM 25:4–5 NCV

If you're lost in the jungle, chances are that intuition alone won't lead you to safety. What you need is a knowledgeable, trustworthy guide—someone who is familiar with the terrain and knows the best route to your final destination.

God is just such a guide. He knows the journey that lies ahead of you. He knows where each decision you make will lead. Ask Him for guidance when you come to any crossroad in life, big or small. With the Bible as your map, its truth as your compass, and God's Spirit as your guide, you can make it through any wilderness—from embarking on a new career to offering loving direction to your children.

I know not the way God leads me,
but well do I know my Guide.

MARTIN LUTHER

YOUR DAILY REFLECTIONS

_____

_____

_____

_____

Jesus said, "Whoever believes in the Son has eternal life."
JOHN 3:36 NRSV

How long is forever? It's a question without an answer that can be humanly comprehended. But, God says that's how long your life will be when you belong to Him. Your life here on Earth is just the beginning, just the childhood of your eternal existence.

Keeping that fact in mind will make a difference in how you choose to live today. It can help balance your priorities as you consider what will last and what will not. It can alleviate your worries about getting older, because there is a new body waiting for you that will never wear out. It can lighten your heart, because there's a time ahead when tears will be a thing of the past.

That's cause for celebration, each and every day, for this moment and forever.

People who dwell in God dwell in the Eternal Now.
MEISTER ECKHART

YOUR DAILY REFLECTIONS

_____

_____

_____

_____

Let us hold fast the confession of our hope without wavering,
for He who promised is faithful.

HEBREWS 10:23

Your body is an amazing creation. It has the ability to move around, to feel a summer breeze, to hear a crack of thunder, to differentiate between the taste of a strawberry and a kiwi.

Taking care of such an incredible masterpiece is a big responsibility. But, despite its complexity, God has kept the maintenance of your body rather simple. Get enough sleep. Eat a balanced diet. Get up and move around on a regular basis. Praise God when you're feeling well. Ask for His help and healing when you're not.

Your body is a gift from God. Why not take a moment right now and thank Him for the miracle He has entrusted into your care?

Take care of your health,
that it may serve you to serve God.

SAINT FRANCIS DE SALES

YOUR DAILY REFLECTIONS

_____

_____

_____

_____

Encourage the timid, help the weak, be patient with everyone.
1 Thessalonians 1:16–17 niv

The word "encourage" means to impart courage to another. Giving others the courage to live up to their potential, overcome obstacles, or even just to hang on to life is a powerful gift. But, that gift comes wrapped in many different ways.

Consider how others have encouraged you. What has been most effective in motivating you to move forward with confidence? Reflect on your own personality and abilities. If you're a verbal person, a phone call or heart-to-heart chat may be the method that works best. If not, writing a note, sharing a hug, or saying a prayer may be more your style.

No matter what method of encouragement you choose, give generously, just as God has sent others to encourage you.

If you wish to be disappointed, look to others.
If you wish to be downhearted, look to yourself.
If you wish to be encouraged, look upon Jesus Christ.
Erich Sauer

YOUR DAILY REFLECTIONS

_____

_____

_____

_____

God affirms us, making us a sure thing in Christ,
putting his Yes within us. By his Spirit he has stamped us
with his eternal pledge—a sure beginning of what he is
destined to complete.

2 CORINTHIANS 1:21–22 THE MESSAGE

You need insurance when you don't have assurance. Without the assurance that other drivers will obey the traffic laws, you need car insurance. Without the assurance that a fire won't ignite in your home, you need homeowner's insurance. You purchase insurance, just in case.

But, when it comes to God, there is no need for a backup plan. You have the assurance that God will never fail. Never. Read the stories of Abraham and Moses in the Old Testament. Take note of how God never failed to come through—even when those who promised to faithfully follow Him did not.

When you give your life to God, you can rest assured—your future is secure.

What a wonderful thing it is to be sure of our faith!

G. F. HANDEL

YOUR DAILY REFLECTIONS

_____

_____

_____

_____

We must not become tired of doing good.
We must not give up.

GALATIANS 6:9 NCV

Reaching any goal in life takes more than just hard work. It takes determination. Determination is a mind-set that is constantly evaluating where you are against where you want to be. It not only helps keep you focused on your goal, but on the reasons behind your desire to reach it. It keeps you moving forward, whether your progress is rocky or smooth.

God wants to help. What objectives, ambitions, or aspirations are you determined to reach in this life? Ask God to help you choose your goals wisely, then move beyond any roadblocks that are slowing your progress. His loving encouragement and perfect perspective are what you need to help you aim high—and not give up.

Be like a postage stamp—
stick to one thing until you get there.

JOSH BILLINGS

YOUR DAILY REFLECTIONS

_____

_____

_____

_____

God sets the lonely in families.

PSALM 68:6 NIV

Families are God's idea. When Jesus came to Earth, even He was part of a family. Though every family is unique, they all share one thing in common. They are the testing ground for true relationship.

Living up close and personal with anyone gives you a chance to discover what love is all about. Joy, sacrifice, comfort, forgiveness, patience, commitment, support—the list goes on and on. What lessons in love can you learn from your family or close friends who act as family?

No matter what role you play in your family, it is irreplaceable. No one else can bring to the people in your life the unique qualities you bring. Ask God to help you carry out your role with honor and integrity.

Loving relationships are a family's best protection
against the challenges of the world.

BERNIE WIEBE

YOUR DAILY REFLECTIONS

You have been saved by grace because you believe.
You did not save yourselves. It was a gift from God.
EPHESIANS 2:8 NCV

Suppose you see some items at the mall that seem to be calling your name. Payday is still a week away, so you whip out your credit card and take those items home. When the bill comes, the credit card company tells you to ignore it and consider the items a gift.

Fantasy? You bet. But, there is a wonderful gift that God has made available to you. His grace is a gift that keeps on giving, when you least deserve it. Unlike credit card companies, God's grace period is eternal. He'll never call in the debt you owe. Jesus has paid it in full. Take a moment to reflect on God's grace. Then, offer Him a gift in return—your thanks.

Grace is love that cares and stoops and rescues.
JOHN STOTT

YOUR DAILY REFLECTIONS

_____

_____

_____

_____

Good people will be guided by honesty.

PROVERBS 11:3 NCV

Honesty is evident in the little things. Pointing out an error on a lunch tab when it happens to be in the restaurant's favor. Being truthful in telling a story when exaggerating it would get a bigger laugh. Or even giving your true weight on your driver's license when it doesn't match the weight you really are going to be once you lose those pesky ten pounds.

An honest heart reflects God's nature. That doesn't mean that honesty happens naturally. It's a character trait that matures over time as you are honest with yourself, with God, and with others. But, the more you practice it, the more natural it feels. Make sure you are growing in honesty each day.

Honesty is the first chapter in the book of wisdom.

THOMAS JEFFERSON

YOUR DAILY REFLECTIONS

_____

_____

_____

_____

*The Spirit himself joins with our spirits to say
that we are God's children.*

ROMANS 8:16 NCV

Your fingerprints are unique designs of arches, loops, and whorls—intricate patterns laid down at birth. Your legal identity is forever linked to them. They never change.

Your spiritual identity, on the other hand, has undergone a rebirth. The day you accepted Jesus as your Lord and Savior and let God's love into your heart, you became a child of God.

Being identified as God's child means that now God's fingerprints can be seen more clearly than ever, all over your life. The result is pure art. Being secure in your identity, enjoying being the person God created you to be, and appreciating the unique place He has given you in this world will help you live every day to the fullest—with childlike abandon and joy.

Everything is good when it leaves the Creator's hands.

JEAN-JACQUES ROUSSEAU

YOUR DAILY REFLECTIONS

_____

_____

_____

_____

We walk by faith, not by sight.

2 CORINTHIANS 5:7 NRSV

Your faith is like a muscle. The more you flex it, the stronger it grows. But, you don't have to don your sweatpants and venture to the gym to get results. All you need to do is recommit yourself every morning to spend time with God, asking Him what He has for you to do in the day ahead.

Acting on what you believe—on what you learn from the Bible, at church, and from God through prayer—keeps your faith in shape. Consider that the things you believe affect your day-to-day life. Is there an area of your life where you need to exercise your faith? Think about it. Pray about it. And then, flex your faith muscle.

Faith is to believe what you do not yet see:
the reward for this faith is to see what you believe.

SAINT AUGUSTINE OF HIPPO

YOUR DAILY REFLECTIONS

_____

_____

_____

_____

It is more blessed to give than to receive.

ACTS 20:35 KJV

Everyone has needs. Sometimes, people have needs they cannot possibly meet by themselves. Praying for them is a good start. But, God also asks you to be His hands and feet, to reach out in a tangible way to help those in need.

First, you have to know who they are. Opening your eyes to look for those in your community, or even around the world, who could use your help is the key to opening your heart. Then, all that is left to do is to open your hands.

What does God want you to do in a world that will always need more than you alone can possibly give? Ask Him. You are only responsible to do your part. But when you do, you'll discover that when you give in God's name, you also will be blessed.

The true source of cheerfulness is benevolence.
The soul that perpetually overflows with kindness
and sympathy will always be cheerful.

PARKE GODWIN

YOUR DAILY REFLECTIONS

_____

_____

_____

_____

He that maketh haste to be rich shall not be innocent.

PROVERBS 28:20 KJV

You are rich. But your net worth isn't determined by the amount of jewelry in your dresser, a BMW in the driveway, or a bank account in Switzerland. That's because the priceless riches you possess can't be lost or sold. They are held securely in your heart.

What riches do you have hidden there? Consider your closest relationships, your fondest memories, the boundless love of your heavenly Father. Riches such as these are sure to only increase in value over time.

When your wealth is found in things that last, your money—and what it can buy—loses its importance. So, invest in what truly matters. Spend time with the people you love.

If you want to feel rich, just count all the things you have that money can't buy.

AUTHOR UNKNOWN

YOUR DAILY REFLECTIONS

_____

_____

_____

_____

Be strong in the Lord and in the power of His might.

EPHESIANS 6:10

When a hurricane hits the coastal waters, winds and waves batter waterfront homes. That's when the strength of a home's construction is put to the test. A solid foundation, attention to accuracy in its construction, and the quality of materials used to build it will all help determine whether the home is still standing when the wind subsides.

When personal storms batter your life, your strength will become evident in much the same way. The truth you've built your life upon, the attention you've given to growing in your faith, and the extent to which you've let God develop the unique qualities He's built into your character will all help you stand strong when the winds begin to blow.

The weaker we feel, the harder we lean on God.
And the harder we lean, the stronger we grow.

JONI EARECKSON TADA

YOUR DAILY REFLECTIONS

_____

_____

_____

_____

Jesus said, "Whenever you stand praying, forgive, if you have
anything against anyone; so that your Father also who is
in heaven may forgive you your transgressions."
LUKE 6:35–36

A grudge is like a rock you choose to haul around with you wherever you go. Though you may feel justified in carrying it, all it really does is weigh you down. Today is the perfect time to get rid of it. That doesn't mean hurling it back at the person who lobbed it at you. All that does it cause more pain.

Instead, take that rock to Jesus. Picture yourself releasing every pebble, or boulder, into His hands—hands strong enough to carry so much more than any person's shoulders can bear. Then, replace that grudge with the feather-light freedom of forgiveness. The heavier the stone you release, the freer you'll feel.

Forgiveness is God's command.
MARTIN LUTHER

YOUR DAILY REFLECTIONS

_____

_____

_____

_____

Jesus said, "Put God's kingdom first.
Do what he wants you to do."

MATTHEW 6:33 NIrV

If you're like most people, your life is a whirlwind of roles and responsibilities. Work schedules, school schedules, vacation schedules, church schedules—it never ends. No wonder it's so difficult to keep your priorities in order. It's tough, but it can be done. The most important step? Remembering to put God first.

Making God your first priority doesn't mean you neglect your kids, your spouse, or your job. Instead, it means turning to God for help as you endeavor to prioritize the demands of your day. It means letting Him help you make the most of every moment.

Ask God to help you focus on what's most important. Then, you can feel confident even in the midst of your busy life.

When you put God first, you are establishing order
for everything else in your life.

ANDREA GARNEY

YOUR DAILY REFLECTIONS

_____

_____

_____

_____

*It is good that a man should both hope and quietly wait
for the salvation of the LORD.*

LAMENTATIONS 3:26 KJV

It isn't easy to focus on what you cannot see. Take parenthood, for instance. Parents have to focus on the future as they raise their children, instilling qualities that will help their children reach their potential. You don't see the results of your work until your kids are much further down the road. But, hope is what keeps you committed to the journey even when things don't look very promising.

Where is hope leading you today? Hope is the fuel that keeps you going, when what you're hoping for is still somewhere down the road. God knows what that is. He's always there to help you refuel. When your tank is low, turn to Him.

Do not look to your hope,
but to Christ, the source of your hope.

CHARLES HADDON SPURGEON

YOUR DAILY REFLECTIONS

_____

_____

_____

_____

Pray and ask God for everything you need.
And when you pray, always give thanks.

PHILIPPIANS 4:6 NCV

Why do you call your friends on the phone? To share exciting news? To ask for advice? Because you enjoy each other's company? Communication is the key to any relationship—whether it's with your friends or the Creator of the universe.

God's line is always open. You'll never receive a busy signal, an answering machine, or get Him out of bed. He's ready to hear it all—your concerns, your questions, your words of thanks. God wants to comfort and encourage you from the inside out and whisper to you the counsel you most need to hear.

He also wants to act on your behalf. Ask God for what you need—physically, spiritually, and emotionally. Whatever is important to you is important enough to become a prayer.

We should speak to God from our own hearts
and talk to him as a child talks to his father.

CHARLES HADDON SPURGEON

YOUR DAILY REFLECTIONS

_____

_____

_____

_____

Honor God by accepting each other,
as Christ has accepted you.

ROMANS 15:7 CEV

At times, life can feel like one big self-improvement program. There is always some habit you could gain more control over, some skill you'd like to perfect, or some character trait you feel could use an extra season of growth. But, in God's eyes, you're already perfect—no matter where you are on the road to maturity.

This very minute, God accepts you exactly the way you are. Certainly, He encourages you to continue to mature. But, knowing you're accepted, no matter what, gives you freedom to be yourself, without reservation. Rejection is not His way. This means you can relax and enjoy your relationship with God. He's loves you just the way you are.

If God accepts me as I am, then I had better do the same.

HUGH MONTEFIORE

YOUR DAILY REFLECTIONS

_____

_____

_____

_____

I want to complete the work the Lord Jesus has given me.
ACTS 20:24 NIrV

Picture yourself on a soccer team. You score a goal. What does everyone on your team do? Cheer, of course. The same is true when you reach a goal in life. God is on your team, cheering you on toward success. However, you can't succeed without first setting a goal. It would be like playing soccer with no designated way to score. What would be the point?

Making your life count means working toward goals that God helps you set. Break down large goals into smaller action steps. Periodically, reevaluate your progress. Celebrate interim victories. Turn to God for encouragement, if you get tired along the way. Then, keep moving forward with expectation. Your goal is within reach.

You become successful the moment
you start moving toward a worthwhile goal.
AUTHOR UNKNOWN

YOUR DAILY REFLECTIONS

_____

_____

_____

_____

No matter what happens, always be thankful.

1 THESSALONIANS 5:18 NLT

Having a thankful heart means more than just being a "glass half full" kind of person. Instead, it means going through your day with such a deep sense of God's presence that you are aware of the part He plays in the details of your life.

Making a conscious effort to see how God takes even difficult circumstances and uses them in positive ways is one way of nurturing this attitude of gratitude. Getting in the habit of saying "thanks" is another.

Take time right now to reflect on what God's given you in the physical sense. Ask Him to open your eyes to even more reasons for thanks. Then, spend a moment thanking Him for how He's at work behind the scenes.

Thou has given so much to me.
Give me one thing more—a grateful heart.

GEORGE HERBERT

YOUR DAILY REFLECTIONS

_____

_____

_____

_____

The Lord searches all the earth for people who have given themselves completely to him.

2 CHRONICLES 16:9 NCV

Keeping your promises isn't easy. Things come up. You lose interest. What you said you'd do ends up being inconvenient or unpleasant. But, making a commitment—and following through with it—lets those around you know that you are a person of your word. You can be trusted.

Consider your biggest commitments. They may include doing your work with excellence, loving your spouse unconditionally, raising your children lovingly, and following God faithfully. Putting your whole heart into these endeavors over the long haul isn't an easy task. But, God can help you make good on your commitments, one day at a time until the job is done.

The moment one definitely commits oneself, the Providence moves too. All sorts of things occur to help that would never otherwise have occurred.

W. H. MURRAY

YOUR DAILY REFLECTIONS

_____

_____

_____

_____

Jesus said, Blessed are they that mourn:
for they shall be comforted.

MATTHEW 5:4 KJV

Where do you turn when you find yourself anxious, worried, discouraged, or in pain? There is an endless list of "comforters" people like to turn to—television, sports, shopping, food. But, God is the only comforter who does more than cover up the uncomfortable. God's comfort also heals.

Whatever grieves your heart grieves the heart of the One who loves you. Turning your worries into prayers allows God to put His arms around you, often in unexpected ways. Whether you find God's comfort in renewed peace of mind, joy in His creation, or companionship from someone God's placed in your life, let God soothe your soul today in ways that comfort food and mindless distractions never will.

No affliction nor temptation, no guilt nor power of sin, no wounded spirit nor terrified conscience should induce us to despair of help and comfort from God!

THOMAS SCOTT

YOUR DAILY REFLECTIONS

_____

_____

_____

_____

Surely goodness and mercy shall follow me
all the days of my life:
and I will dwell in the house of the LORD for ever.

PSALM 23:6 KJV

Fast-food advertising urges you to take a break. And why not? You deserve it. You've worked hard, whether inside or outside your home. But, God wants to give you a break you don't deserve. It's called mercy.

God's gift of mercy means you have a future home in Heaven that you don't deserve. It means there's no reason to beat yourself up over bad choices you've made in the past. God's mercy has granted you a complete pardon.

Mercy is more than a lucky break. Mercy is a gift of love. Extending it to others when they least deserve it is a way you can let God's love work through you.

Mercy is compassion in action.

AUTHOR UNKNOWN

YOUR DAILY REFLECTIONS

_____

_____

_____

_____

The righteous will never be moved. …
Their hearts are firm, secure in the LORD.

PSALM 112:6–7 NRSV

In an earthquake, what once was solid and secure beneath your feet may suddenly buckle and collapse. But, not all earthquakes take place in the earth's crust. They can also occur in relationships, with a doctor's diagnosis, or with the appearance of a pink slip at work.

How do you calm a frightened heart when your world begins to shake? Just like a crying child knows that safety is as close as her mother's arms, you have the assurance that God is a safe place to turn. He is your strong tower, your solid rock, your safe haven. Rest in Him. Even if the world around you is falling apart, He stands firm.

No matter what may be the test,
God will take care of you.

C. D. MARTIN

YOUR DAILY REFLECTIONS

_____

_____

_____

_____

*Set an example for the believers in speech, in life,
in love, in faith and in purity.*

1 TIMOTHY 4:12 NIV

The strength of your character is most evident when things don't go your way. When someone cuts you off in traffic. When you don't get the raise you expected. When your teenager makes choices you don't approve of. When you're placed in an awkward position by a friend or family member.

Who you are at your worst and your best is the sum of your true character. God is molding that character day by day to look more like His. As you allow Him to work through the circumstances of your life, He's softening your heart, strengthening your love, and deepening your resolve to follow Him. Now, there's a makeover bound to improve with age.

God is more concerned about our character than
our comfort. His goal is not to pamper us physically
but to perfect us spiritually.

PAUL W. POWELL

YOUR DAILY REFLECTIONS

_____

_____

_____

_____

We know that God is always at work
for the good of everyone who loves him.

ROMANS 8:28 CEV

There are plenty of magazines, television ads, and books out there vying for your attention, each promising to help you live the "good life." The truth is, the good life is already yours. Every day, God sends good gifts your way. He also takes your present circumstances, both good and not-so-good, and uses them to make a positive difference in your life.

Everything that is truly good reflects God's character and plan. So, enjoy the good life to the fullest. Delight in the taste of a freshly picked peach. Rejoice at the sight of your child's first steps. Give thanks for the friend who makes you laugh. A very good God loves you deeply and wishes you nothing but the best.

God is all that is good,
and the goodness that everything has is his.

JULIAN OF NORWICH

YOUR DAILY REFLECTIONS

_____

_____

_____

_____

> *I waited patiently for the Lord.*
> *He turned to me and heard my cry.*
>
> PSALM 40:1 NCV

Life has plenty of waiting rooms, most of them without walls. Waiting for the right spouse to come along. Waiting to see the results of a new exercise program. Waiting for God to answer a desperate prayer.

When you find yourself in a waiting room, you have two choices. You can be patient or impatient. The choice you make won't do anything to change your circumstances. The only thing it can change is you.

Practicing patience begins by accepting that God is in control—and you're not. This frees you to go on with your life while you wait, knowing God's answers will come in His own perfect timing. As your patience grows, you'll find that your trust will grow as well.

Be patient toward all that is unsolved in your heart.

DAG HAMMARSKJÖLD

YOUR DAILY REFLECTIONS

_____

_____

_____

_____

God loves a cheerful giver.

2 CORINTHIANS 9:7 NASB

When an actor is preparing for a role, he or she asks, "What's my motivation?" When preparing to give a gift to others—whether it's a birthday gift for a friend or a check to your local charity—it's helpful to ask yourself that same question.

There are plenty of reasons why people give. Some believe God will give to them more generously if they share what they have. Others enjoy the recognition they get for their generosity. Still others give out of guilt or just because they believe it's the "right" thing to do.

When you give cheerfully, motivated by love, the value of your gift increases. You please God, as well as bless the one you're giving to.

Whatever we hold to ourselves is loss.
Whatever we give to God is gain.

GILBERT SHAW

YOUR DAILY REFLECTIONS

_____

_____

_____

_____

Jesus said, "Peace I leave with you, My peace I give to you;
not as the world gives do I give to you.
Let not your heart be troubled, neither let it be afraid."

JOHN 14:27

When your son is ready to get his driver's permit, your boss is demanding more than you feel you're able to give, or your best friend has been diagnosed with cancer, peace of mind can be hard to find—if you don't know where to look.

Look to God. Recall His faithfulness to you in the past. Look again at what He's promised in the Bible. Consider how much He loves you and those you love. And think about how great His wisdom is, compared to your understanding.

When you have a clear picture of who God is, you'll be able to find great peace—even when life seems a great deal less than peaceful.

Peace comes not by establishing a calm outward setting
so much as by inwardly surrendering
to whatever the setting.

HUBERT VAN ZELLER

YOUR DAILY REFLECTIONS

_____

_____

_____

_____

Let us then approach the throne of grace with confidence,
so that we may receive mercy and find grace
to help us in our time of need.

HEBREWS 4:16 NIV

Confident people carry an air of success with them wherever they go. While having confidence in your own talents, abilities, and experience is important, it's not enough to ensure success—or even a positive self-image. That's because being self-assured can never take the place of being God-assured.

There is confidence to be found in knowing who God says you are and what He's promised to do through you. It's a much better edge than predicting what you can accomplish by your own willpower.

You matter to God. He is working through you to make a difference in this world, just by encouraging you to be yourself. Being confident of that fact is all the confidence you will ever need to succeed.

The greater and more persistent your confidence in God,
the more abundantly you will receive all that you ask.

ALBERT THE GREAT

YOUR DAILY REFLECTIONS

_____

_____

_____

_____

O Lord, you are faithful to those who are faithful to you.
2 Samuel 22:26 GNT

God's forgiveness is without end. At times, that fact can make being faithful to God seem not as important as it should be. After all, no matter what you do, God will forgive you.

But, being faithful is more than just showing up for church on Sundays. Following through on what you know God wants you to do reflects a heart of faithfulness that blesses God and benefits you. It's like when you were a young person in school—the more faithful you were in doing your homework, the more you learned. The same is true of your relationship with God and your own personal maturity. The more you put into it, the more you'll grow. The more faithful you are, the more faithful you'll desire to be.

We know that our rewards depend not on the job itself but on the faithfulness with which we serve God.
John Paul I

YOUR DAILY REFLECTIONS

_____

_____

_____

_____

*Jesus said, "Give your entire attention to what God is doing
right now, and don't get worked up about
what may or may not happen tomorrow."*

MATTHEW 6:34 THE MESSAGE

Multitasking is pretty much a necessity these days—no matter what your job description. You have probably even learned to talk on the phone while cooking or even taking care of small errands and tasks around town. While it's beneficial to be able to handle multiple tasks, handling more than one day at a time is another story altogether.

God wisely broke down life into twenty-four hour periods. He knew a single day was enough to focus on at one time. After all, no one but God really knows what tomorrow may hold.

So, give today all you've got. Ask Him to help you release any worries you have about the future, so you can put your whole heart into the tasks and relationships before you today.

The only light on the future is faith.

THEODOR HOECKER

YOUR DAILY REFLECTIONS

Trust in the LORD with all your heart.
Do not depend on your own understanding.
PROVERBS 3:5 NIrV

When you trust a friend, you will listen to their advice, freely share your deepest secrets, and continue to love that friend, even if you don't always understand everything about them. Well, God is even more trustworthy than your most faithful friend.

That doesn't mean trusting Him is always easy. It can be hard to trust Someone you can't see or easily hear, Someone who asks you to do things you might never have dreamed up on your own. But, God is totally worthy of your trust. Whatever He asks you to do, He will faithfully help you accomplish. When God leads you in a direction that's out of your comfort zone, it isn't a risk to follow Him. It's the only wise way to go.

Trust in God and you are never to be confounded
in time or in eternity.
DWIGHT LYMAN MOODY

YOUR DAILY REFLECTIONS

_____

_____

_____

_____

Whoever walks in integrity walks securely.

PROVERBS 10:9 NRSV

If your private life suddenly became public knowledge, would it make a difference in the way you lived? A person of integrity doesn't keep skeletons in the closet. That doesn't mean you never make mistakes. It just means that you confess them to God, accept His forgiveness, and keep moving forward.

Becoming a person of integrity means making decisions, publicly and privately, that honor God. It means you're the same person, no matter whom you're with. It means turning your back on hidden motives, false pretense, and deception. Leading a life of integrity means being honest about whom you are right now, while working humbly with God to mature into the person He created you to be. Why would you settle for less?

Integrity is not a conditional word.
It doesn't blow in the wind or change with the weather.

JOHN D. MACDONALD

YOUR DAILY REFLECTIONS

_____

_____

_____

_____

I have learned to be content with whatever I have.

PHILIPPIANS 4:11 NRSV

When you haven't had a raise in two years, or the scale says you haven't lost a pound after two weeks of dieting, or you're watching your neighbors head off to the Bahamas when you haven't had a vacation in years, contentment may seem out of reach. But, God wants to help you be truly contented no matter what your circumstances might be.

Anytime you feel a twinge of discontent creeping into your heart, stop it before it takes root. Ask God to help you take a fresh look at what He's doing in your life. Reflect on your reasons to be thankful. Then, thank God for every reason He brings to mind. True contentment begins by choosing to trust and enjoy God's choices for your life.

The secret of contentment is the realization that life
is a gift, not a right.

AUTHOR UNKNOWN

YOUR DAILY REFLECTIONS

_____

_____

_____

_____

God is love. Whoever lives in love lives in God,
and God lives in him.

1 JOHN 4:16 NCV

Want to know what God wants you to do with your life? Love. Love Him. Love others. Love yourself. Doing those three things fulfills every desire God has for you.

Loving well means getting to know others well. It means being aware of their needs, their wounds, their strengths, and their weaknesses—knowing what makes them smile. This includes knowing both God and yourself as well.

How you express your love is unique. Just like there has never been another person exactly like you, there has also never been another expression of love quite like yours. Be creative. Be generous. Be persistent. Be forgiving. Love with the same enthusiasm with which God loves you.

I have found the paradox that if I love until it hurts, then there is no hurt, but only more love.

MOTHER TERESA

YOUR DAILY REFLECTIONS

_____

_____

_____

_____

He puts a little of heaven in our hearts
so that we'll never settle for less.

2 Corinthians 5:5 The Message

Right now, your heart is longing for a home you've never seen. You may not even be aware of this longing, but you feel it every time injustice seems to win out in the world, every time someone you love faces death, every time you're tempted to ask God "why?"

There's no confusing the present world with the eternal home that awaits you. But, that doesn't mean you can't enjoy a taste right now. Close your eyes. Think about meeting Jesus face-to-face. Contemplate a new earth where pollution hasn't taken a toll, where evil has been erased. Imagine a place without tears!

None of us really knows what Heaven will be like. But, one thing is certain—you'll feel right at home.

Heaven will be the perfection we have always longed for.
All the things that made earth unlovely and tragic
will be absent in heaven.

Billy Graham

YOUR DAILY REFLECTIONS

_____

_____

_____

_____

The Spirit of God has made me;
the breath of the Almighty gives me life.

JOB 33:4 NIV

Every person's life is a masterpiece. Yours is no exception. When you're standing close to the canvas, it may look like a series of unrelated splashes of color—a bright spot here, a dark spot there. But, when God looks at your life, He sees the big picture. He wants to help you keep the beauty of that finished artwork in mind as you go through the individual brush stroke called "today."

What color is on the current brush of your life? No matter what hue it may be, God can use it in a vibrant, creative way. Watch Him blend sorrow with joy, difficulty with growth. His palette is always perfect. His design, always unique. His plan for your life, always good.

Life is a great big canvas;
throw all the paint on it you can.

DANNY KAYE

YOUR DAILY REFLECTIONS

_____

_____

_____

_____

Forgive anyone who does you wrong,
just as Christ has forgiven you.

COLOSSIANS 3:13 CEV

A re you reluctant to forgive someone who has hurt or offended you, because it seems like you would be letting that person off the hook? In truth, the only person you would be letting off the hook is you!

Anger, bitterness, and resentment—the natural by-products of unforgiveness—can tie you up in knots. Give them free reign, and you'll soon find that you've done nothing to alleviate the pain you feel and everything to magnify it.

God loves you—that's why He urges you to forgive the offenses that come your way. Let them go. Distance yourself from them. In that way, you strip them of their power to do additional harm and you place yourself squarely in the path of healing.

To forgive is to set a prisoner free
and discover the prisoner was you.

AUTHOR UNKNOWN

YOUR DAILY REFLECTIONS

_____

_____

_____

_____

The LORD will be your confidence,
and will keep your foot from being caught.

PROVERBS 3:26

Wouldn't it be a tragedy if you failed to reach your full potential in life or never realized your dreams and desires—simply because you lacked confidence? Yes, it would! Especially since God says it's possible to have all the confidence you need.

The secret is to know who you are—God's precious and unique child. He created you in His own image; therefore, you are of great personal worth. He promises to be with you always—guiding you, watching over you, making His resources available to you. With His help, you can overcome any obstacle that stands in your path.

God has empowered you to fulfill your destiny. Put your trust in Him, and walk confidently into the future.

Nothing can be done without hope and confidence.

HELEN KELLER

YOUR DAILY REFLECTIONS

_____

_____

_____

_____

You must hold on, so you can do what God wants
and receive what he has promised.

HEBREWS 10:36 NCV

Perseverance—the power to stick with something until it is completed—is the key to achieving your goals and reaching your dreams. No matter how much talent, skill, intelligence, or personal charisma you have, you won't get where you want to go unless you're determined to keep your eyes focused squarely on the finish line.

Persevering means refusing to become distracted by bumps in the road—such as discouraging circumstances. It means discarding the negative opinions and comments of others.

God created you for a purpose, and He wants to see you succeed. When you call on Him, He promises to renew your strength. He was there at the beginning of your race, and He'll be there at the end—so persevere!

There must be a beginning to any great matter, but the continuing to the end until it be thoroughly finished yields the true glory.

THOMAS CARLYLE

YOUR DAILY REFLECTIONS

_____

_____

_____

> LORD, *who may dwell in your sanctuary?*
> *Who may live on your holy hill?*
> *He ... who keeps his oath even when it hurts.*
> PSALM 15:1–2, 4 NIV

Keeping your commitments means doing what you say you're going to do—not *some* of the time, but *all* of the time. That isn't always easy with busy schedules and changing circumstances. But, if you want the respect and trust of others, it's imperative.

The best approach is to make commitments only after carefully considering whether you will be able to fulfill them. Too often, commitments are made quickly, in the heat of the moment, leaving you to discover too late that they are simply impossible to keep.

Let God be your example when it comes to commitments—He always keeps His. He puts the resources of Heaven and Earth behind every commitment He's made to you in the Scriptures.

He who lightly assents will seldom keep his word.
CHINESE PROVERB

YOUR DAILY REFLECTIONS

_____

_____

_____

_____

God began doing a good work in you. And he will continue it
until it is finished when Jesus Christ comes again.

PHILIPPIANS 1:6 NCV

Imagine waiting with great expectation to see the newest canvas of a world-renowned painter, your eyes prepared to behold greatness. This is how you should think of yourself. After all, you were crafted by the Master Artist—God Himself. What greatness will the eyes of others see when the canvas of your life is complete?

Maybe your life, your gifts, your personality, your looks, your resources seem ordinary and commonplace to you. But commit them to God, and you will soon find that they are exploding with promise and opportunity. Enhanced by the fingertips of God, the final result is certain to be extraordinary, special, unique—a true masterpiece. Expect it and you won't be disappointed.

We block Christ's advance in our lives
by failure of expectation.

WILLIAM TEMPLE

YOUR DAILY REFLECTIONS

_____

_____

_____

_____

We are God's workmanship, created in Christ Jesus to do good works, which God prepared in advance for us to do.

EPHESIANS 2:10 NIV

Have you ever been introduced to someone in a way that indicated your relationship to someone else? Maybe you were identified as "Bob's assistant," "Doug's friend," "Daniel's mom." Such descriptions seldom provide a picture of the real you.

But, there is one such identification you might be pleased to have others make. That is your status as a child of God. Can you imagine someone introducing you by saying, "She's full of love and peace—just like her Father God" or "He's artistic—just like his heavenly Father"?

Let your relationship with God provide the greatest part of your personal identity. What more wonderful identity could there be than being His child?

The way in which we think of ourselves has everything to do with how our world sees us.

ARLENE RAVEN

YOUR DAILY REFLECTIONS

_____

_____

_____

_____

It is better to take refuge in the LORD than to trust in man.

PSALM 118:8 NIV

In these treacherous times, it's difficult to know whom you can trust. But there is Someone you can trust unequivocally—that Someone is God. People will fail you, but He never will. He is completely worthy of your trust.

God does not promise that you will never encounter difficult situations or painful circumstances. But He does promise that they will never be more than the two of you, together, can manage. He also promises that good will come from any and every situation that touches your life—even heartache and tragedy. And most wonderful of all—He says that nothing will be able to separate you from His love.

Place your trust in God. He always keeps His promises.

I have held many things in my hands,
and I have lost them all; but whatever I have placed
in God's hands, that I still possess.

CORRIE TEN BOOM

YOUR DAILY REFLECTIONS

_____

_____

_____

_____

If we confess our sins, He is faithful and just to forgive us
our sins and to cleanse us from all unrighteousness.

1 JOHN 1:9

You may find it difficult to forget your mistakes, your missteps, your sins. But God doesn't—He forgives *and* forgets. Imagine a piece of paper filled with confessions of your past indiscretions. Suppose every single sin you ever committed appeared on that page. Like a child might hand a paper with a bad grade to his or her parent, you reluctantly give the list of your sins to God.

God takes that paper and crumples it into a tiny ball. Then He throws it into a burning fire—it is consumed— never to be remembered again.

God's forgiveness is just like that. Once He has forgiven you, He will never bring it up again—so why would you? Go on your way and sin no more!

Forgiveness does not mean the cancellation of all
consequences of wrongdoing. It means the refusal
on God's part to let our guilty past affect
His relationship with us.

AUTHOR UNKNOWN

YOUR DAILY REFLECTIONS

_____

_____

_____

_____

*You have begun to live the new life. In your new life,
you are being made new. You are becoming like
the One who made you.*

COLOSSIANS 3:10 NCV

In the midst of life's challenges, God gives you a wonderful gift—a fresh start. No matter what choices you have made in the past, turning over your mistakes to God will put you on the path to a bright future.

Think about it this way: a house shows signs of past abuse, neglect, and turbulent weather. The painter comes along and strips off the old peeling paint, sands the boards, and applies a fresh, clean coat of paint. Signs of the past are gone for good, and the house has a fresh new start.

Likewise, God has given you the honor and privilege of being able to shake off past mistakes and experience a fresh start. He is the God of new beginnings.

If you have made mistakes, even serious ones,
there is always another chance for you. What we call
failure is not the falling down, but the staying down.

MARY PICKFORD

YOUR DAILY REFLECTIONS

_____

_____

_____

_____

The plans of the diligent lead surely to plenty.

PROVERBS 21:5

God created the entire universe in six days, and as each part was completed, He looked it over and said, "It is good." He undertook His work with diligence and was rewarded with a sense of satisfaction.

God wants you to gain satisfaction in return for your diligence as well—and you can. No matter what task lies before you, you have the power to transform it from being an exhausting struggle to a creative joy, simply by changing the way you view it.

Take a second look at the task at hand—reconciling your checkbook, changing diapers, or traveling on a long flight to a business meeting. Ask God to open your eyes to the creative energy in that task. Then go about it with your whole heart. You'll enjoy your work a whole lot more, and God will bless you for it.

God is the Best and Most Orderly Workman of all.

COPERNICUS

YOUR DAILY REFLECTIONS

_____

_____

_____

_____

*Children are a heritage from the Lord, the fruit of
the womb a reward. As arrows are in the hand of a warrior,
so are the children of one's youth.*

PSALM 127:3–4 AMP

When Jesus was here on Earth, He often took time for children. He held them, blessed them, and told His disciples that their tender innocence and simple faith were the essence of the Kingdom of God.

If you have children, you no doubt know that God has entrusted you with a most precious treasure. He expects you to give them your very best and raise them with an understanding of His goodness and grace.

Just as an archer aims and then shoots an arrow toward his target, God has given you the ability to direct and send forth your children. And He has also given you His word that He will be there to help you, every step of the way.

Children must be valued as our most priceless possession.

JAMES DOBSON

YOUR DAILY REFLECTIONS

_____

_____

_____

_____

God's mercy is so abundant, and his love for us is so great,
that while we were spiritually dead
in our disobedience he brought us to life with Christ.

EPHESIANS 2:4–5 GNT

Before you ever thought about Him, a merciful God loved you and executed a plan to redeem your life. His goodness and mercy defeated sin and judgment and opened the way of peace for you. That mercy is available to you every day.

If you feel you have failed God, His mercy will free you from guilt and condemnation. If you feel you have failed someone else, His mercy will be upon you as you seek to make things right. And God's mercy will always be available for you to pass along to others.

We all need mercy—both to give and to receive. God is the source. Look to Him and He will give you all you need.

Nothing graces the Christian soul as much as mercy.

SAINT AMBROSE

YOUR DAILY REFLECTIONS

_____

_____

_____

_____

When you talk, do not say harmful things.
But say what people need—
words that will help others become stronger.

EPHESIANS 4:29 NCV

God's spoken words were powerful enough to create the universe. You were made in His image; therefore, your words have power too—the power to hurt or heal, encourage or condemn, safeguard the truth or foster lies.

God wants you to use your words in the same way He does—for good. It will mean a decision of your will and a lot of determination, but your words can make you a creative force for good in the world.

Ask God to help you take charge of your tongue and thus control the power of your spoken words. God's words created the universe and all it contains. Imagine the wonderful things your words can do.

Little keys can open big locks. Simple words
can express great thoughts.

WILLIAM ARTHUR WARD

YOUR DAILY REFLECTIONS

_____

_____

_____

_____

*Blessed be the God and Father of our Lord Jesus Christ,
which according to his abundant mercy hath begotten us again
unto a lively hope by the resurrection of Jesus Christ from
the dead, to an inheritance incorruptible, and undefiled,
and that fadeth not away, reserved in heaven for you.*

1 PETER 1:3–4 KJV

Heaven is the home God has prepared for those He has redeemed through His Son, Jesus Christ. It's a real place—a place full of God's perfect love, joy, and peace. There is no pain there, no tears. So grand is it that the Bible only reveals small glimpses of its marvels.

One day you will see Heaven and all its magnificence. Until then, there is only one way to experience a *taste* of Heaven right here on Earth—that is by spending time in sweet communion with God.

Spending eternity in Heaven is indeed something to anticipate. But until you can walk its streets, get into God's presence and treat yourself to a *taste* of what your future holds.

Blessed assurance, Jesus is mine!
O what a foretaste of glory divine!

FANNY CROSBY

YOUR DAILY REFLECTIONS

_____

_____

_____

God will cover you with his wings; you will be safe in his care;
his faithfulness will protect and defend you.

PSALM 91:4 GNT

Try to remember a time as a child when you were frightened by a storm in the night. You probably called out to your parents or even crawled into bed with them. As you felt the warmth of their embrace and listened to their comforting words, you went right back to sleep—quickly forgetting the storm that continued to rage just outside the window.

God—your heavenly Father—wants to be your Comforter and Protector today. He has even commissioned His angels to guard you at all times, and He has promised to never leave you alone or forsake you. As you meditate on these truths, your heart will be warmed and you will be at peace.

Commit yourself to His loving care. He's always watching over you.

Prayer is the key that shuts us up under
his protection and safeguard.

JACQUES ELLUL

YOUR DAILY REFLECTIONS

_____

_____

_____

_____

*Jesus said, "If you have faith as a mustard seed,
you can say to this mulberry tree, 'Be pulled up by the roots
and be planted in the sea,' and it would obey you."*

LUKE 17:6

Imagine a man or woman who wants to participate in a long bicycle trip, but hasn't ridden in years. On the first day, the person in question can only ride half a mile. But each day, the person is able to go a little further. Soon, leg muscles begin to grow strong and the individual is able to ride the bike for ten miles.

Faith can be compared to those leg muscles. It also grows strong with exercise. God has given you the ability to believe, to love, to acknowledge Him. And as you take one small step at a time in His direction, believing His Word, your faith will grow stronger and stronger. Soon, you will be achieving things you never dreamed possible.

Faith is nothing at all tangible.
It is simply believing God.

HANNAH WHITHALL SMITH

YOUR DAILY REFLECTIONS

_____

_____

_____

_____

You are a chosen race, a royal priesthood, a dedicated nation,
[God's] own purchased, special people.

1 PETER 2:9 AMP

The desire for acceptance is very human. We long for it, seek it, and do all we can to acquire it. With some people the need goes so deep that it colors every aspect of their lives—what they wear, how they speak, where they go, even their opinions and behaviors.

How sad that these people have never discovered that God loves and accepts them just as they are. Don't let that be said of you. After all, God created you. You are precious and priceless in His sight. You have *His* seal of approval.

If you are desperately seeking acceptance, look to God. Ask Him to show you what He sees in you. Once you see yourself as He sees you, your search will be over.

Accept the fact that you are accepted.

PAUL TILLICH

YOUR DAILY REFLECTIONS

_____

_____

_____

_____

> *I bless the LORD who gives me counsel;*
> *in the night also my heart instructs me.*
>
> PSALM 16:7 NRSV

Each day, you are faced with decisions that must be made—and made well, because each one will affect your life and the lives of those around you. How can you guarantee that you'll always choose wisely? You can't. You're human, and you're going to make mistakes from time to time. But there are ways to increase your odds.

First, avoid making decisions based primarily on emotion. Feelings can cloud your judgment. Second, become informed. Before you make up your mind, gather as much pertinent information as possible. Third, ask God to infuse your knowledge with His wisdom and to follow that up with His peace. When you've considered the facts and feel God's peace, your decisions are apt to be ones you can live with.

> Yes and no are the two most important words
> that you will ever say. These are the two words
> that determine your destiny in life.
>
> AUTHOR UNKNOWN

YOUR DAILY REFLECTIONS

_____

_____

_____

O Lord my God, I will give you thanks forever.
PSALM 30:12 NIV

Life is full of things to be grateful for—small acts of kindness and generosity, words of hope and encouragement, gifts of love and caring. Look around you and see how many you can count in just a few moments.

Perhaps on your way to work you passed a tree full of lovely spring blossoms. Or one of your coworkers brought you a cup of coffee. Or your spouse gave you a long embrace before leaving the house. It could be that you were kissed by a child, snuggled by a kitten, comforted by a touch.

A thankful heart takes time to notice those small, precious gifts. Are you thankful for the little things that come your way? Why don't you let God know.

Thanksgiving is good but thanks-living is better.
MATTHEW HENRY

YOUR DAILY REFLECTIONS

_____

_____

_____

_____

The wisdom from above is first pure, then peaceable,
gentle, willing to yield, full of mercy and good fruits,
without a trace of partiality or hypocrisy.

JAMES 3:17 NRSV

Imagine purchasing something that has "Assembly required" on the label. Now think about getting out the tools, parts, and directions for the project, only to discover that a picture of the finished product has not been included. That's the way some situations in your life can seem. That's why you need God's wisdom to pull it all together.

God's wisdom sees the big picture and gives you perspective. It may help you to see options that were not apparent before. And His wisdom can help you make good choices.

Life is tricky. God wants you to go forward with everything you need for success. That includes the big picture that only He can provide.

Men may acquire knowledge,
but wisdom is a gift direct from God.

BOB JONES

YOUR DAILY REFLECTIONS

_____

_____

_____

_____

Behold, how good and how pleasant it is for brethren
to dwell together in unity!

PSALM 133:1

Do you know a person who seems to have an abundance of friends? Look closely and you'll probably notice that person reaching out, initiating toward others, and cultivating new relationships.

Too often people sit around waiting for others to come to them. But friendship, like most valuable things in life, requires an investment of time and effort. If you want it, you must be willing to work for it.

If you'd like to have more friends, go out and get them. Practice those virtues that you feel a good friend would have. Be an encourager and an attentive listener. Show an interest in other people. Soon you'll be wondering how you're going to find time for all the new people in your life.

The only way to have a friend is to be a friend.

RALPH WALDO EMERSON

YOUR DAILY REFLECTIONS

_____

_____

_____

_____

This is the testimony: God has given us eternal life,
and this life is in his Son. He who has the Son has life;
he who does not have the Son of God does not have life.
1 JOHN 5:11–12 NIV

Eternal life isn't just living forever in Heaven with God—although that's certainly part of it. Your promise for eternal life includes the here and now. If you've entrusted yourself to God's care and received His gift of salvation, you have the reality of eternal life today. You don't have to wait to die an earthly death before you can enjoy it.

The Bible says that God's goodness and mercy will follow you all the days of your life. So why live another day without hope, without joy, without meaning. Reach out to God. Trade in your old life for a new one, and start living life to the fullest—all the days of your life here on Earth—and later in Heaven.

The life of faith does not earn eternal life;
it is eternal life.
WILLIAM TEMPLE

YOUR DAILY REFLECTIONS

_____

_____

_____

_____

I will send down showers in season;
there will be showers of blessing.

EZEKIEL 34:26 NIV

Parents know what a pleasant feeling it is to indulge their children with gifts—so pleasant that they often have to restrain themselves for their children's own good. Your heavenly Father loves to pour out gifts and blessings on His children too. Look around and you'll see the wonderful things He's already placed in your life.

Notice the finger-painted sunrise God made just for you. Consider the joy, love, comfort, encouragement, and caring that God has poured out on you through your friends and family members. Then close your eyes and meditate on the greatest blessing of all—that God loves you. Thank your Father for all of your many blessings. Your love and thanks bless Him in return.

God is more anxious to bestow his blessings on us
than we are to receive them.

SAINT AUGUSTINE OF HIPPO

YOUR DAILY REFLECTIONS

_____

_____

_____

_____

The character of even a child can be known by the way
he acts—whether what he does is pure and right.

PROVERBS 20:11 TLB

Character is commonly defined as moral strength—the ability to consistently do the right thing for the right reasons. How do you stack up when it comes to character?

You may already be a person whose strength of character is well established. But, if you aren't, you can be. No matter what you have done in the past, you have an opportunity each day to do what is right; and each time you do what is right, you plant a seed of character in your life.

Add to that one more ingredient—endurance. As you sustain a pattern of choosing to do what is right, you will be well on your way to becoming the strong person of character God has always intended you to be.

We first make our habits, then our habits make us.

JOHN DRYDEN

YOUR DAILY REFLECTIONS

_____

_____

_____

_____

God wanted to have many sons share his glory.
So God made perfect the One who leads people to salvation.
He made Jesus a perfect Savior through Jesus' suffering.

HEBREWS 2:10 NCV

God's desire to have a family—a group of people related to each other—is the reason He created man. He desired the fellowship of many sons and daughters and began with Adam and Eve. When Adam and Eve fell, God's family was in jeopardy of remaining separated from Him for eternity.

God loves His family even more than any man or woman could love theirs. So, He sent Jesus, His only Son, to reunite Himself with His family once again. When you choose to cross the bridge created by Jesus' death and triumphant resurrection, you become a child of the Most High God and join a family like none you have ever known.

God and man exist for each other
and neither is satisfied without the other.

A. W. TOZER

YOUR DAILY REFLECTIONS

_____

_____

_____

_____

Riches and honor come from you, and you rule over all.
In your hand are power and might; and it is in your hand
to make great and to give strength to all.

1 CHRONICLES 29:12 NRSV

Whether you have plenty of money or not enough, chances are you spend a lot of time thinking about it. Where should you invest your excess? Where can you come up with the difference between what you have and what you need? In both cases, God is available to help. He can bring wisdom to your efforts and help you keep financial issues in proper perspective.

Begin by recognizing God as your Source—your Provider. All you have now and all you will ever have come from Him.

If you have more than enough, ask God to help you be a good steward of what He has given you. If you have too little, ask Him to help you find ways to make up the difference.

There is no portion of money that is our money and the rest God's money. It is all his; he made it all, gives it all, and he has simply trusted it to us for his service.

ADOLPHE MONOD

YOUR DAILY REFLECTIONS

_____

_____

_____

All have sinned and fall short of the glory of God,
and are justified freely by his grace through the redemption
that came by Christ Jesus.

ROMANS 3:23 NIV

Are you struggling with a situation in your life in which you feel you were unjustly treated? Have you been wondering if God knows or cares? The Bible says that He does, and He will see that justice is done in your case. But remember this: God's justice is carried out in His own time and in His own way.

God's justice is tempered by His mercy and His understanding of what is best for each person in His care. He will not rush to judgment. He is patient even with those who err. The good news is that at some point, in another situation, that person may be you.

Don't allow bitterness to control your life. Commit yourself to God, and trust Him to deal justly and mercifully on your behalf.

The pearl of justice is found in the heart of mercy.

SAINT CATHERINE OF SIENA

YOUR DAILY REFLECTIONS

_____

_____

_____

_____

The very God of peace sanctify you wholly; and I pray God
your whole spirit and soul and body be preserved blameless
unto the coming of our Lord Jesus Christ.

1 THESSALONIANS 5:23 KJV

God created you in His image. That means you are triune—a spirit being who lives in a body and has a mind. He wants you to experience health in every area—each part working in harmony with the others. That's the only way you can become all He has created you to be.

Your spirit can only be nourished and kept healthy as you spend time with God. A healthy mind requires a regular diet of positive thoughts and images. Try the Bible. It's filled with God's words of love and encouragement. A healthy spirit and mind provide a foundation of wisdom and understanding on which to maintain a healthy body.

Don't settle for health in only one part of your being. Ask God to help you pursue wholeness.

To be "whole" is to be spiritually, emotionally, and physically healthy. Jesus lived in perfect wholeness.

COLIN URQUHART

YOUR DAILY REFLECTIONS

_____

_____

_____

_____

Within your temple, O God,
we meditate on your unfailing love.

PSALM 48:9 NIV

A quiet walk by the lake, an hour sitting near the fireplace, or just gathering your thoughts at the kitchen table are all savored times of reflection. They can also be moments alone with God, meditating on the reality of His intervention in your life.

The Bible says that God walked with Adam and Eve in the Garden of Eden. They spent time together in the cool of the evening. God also wants to spend time with you. He longs for you to know Him better, to understand His wonderful plans and purposes for your life. And He wants to hear what you have to say as you meditate on His goodness. Focus your meditation on God. He's always ready to meet you.

Meditation is the activity of calling to mind, and
thinking over, and dwelling on, and applying to oneself,
the various things that one knows about the works
and ways and purposes and promises of God.

J. I. PACKER

YOUR DAILY REFLECTIONS

_____

_____

_____

_____

*We take thought beforehand and aim to be honest
and absolutely above suspicion, not only in the sight
of the Lord but also in the sight of men.*

2 CORINTHIANS 8:21 AMP

Integrity can be defined as uprightness of heart. It is the primary characteristic of a person who regularly and consistently does what is right. Such a person lives an honest life, honors others, and can be counted on to keep commitments. A person of integrity gives 100 percent on the job, and his or her spouse lives securely because he or she can be trusted.

Are you a person of integrity? Does your character set you apart from the crowd? Do you draw a line in the sand and refuse to cross it for any reason? Look at your heart for a moment. With God's help, you can live a life of integrity that is pleasing to Him.

Integrity is the first step to true greatness.

CHARLES SIMMONS

YOUR DAILY REFLECTIONS

_____

_____

_____

_____

*These [miracles] are written that you may believe
that Jesus is the Christ, the Son of God,
and that believing you may have life in His name.*

JOHN 20:31

Belief can be defined as a conviction so firm that a person accepts it as truth—even if it isn't. For that reason, it's important to examine the evidence before believing in any premise—even the existence of God.

Look around you and take in the physical evidence, a world of exquisite beauty and breathtaking detail. Add to that the testimony of others. Ask people why they believe in God, and then evaluate what they have to say. Read the Bible and see what God has to say about Himself. Last of all, ask God to make Himself real to you. Do all the pieces fit?

God encourages an honest search for truth. He wants you to be certain that your belief in Him is well placed.

The point of having an open mind, like having
an open mouth, is to close it on something solid.

G. K. CHESTERTON

YOUR DAILY REFLECTIONS

_____

_____

_____

_____

*Birds find nooks and crannies in your house, sparrows
and swallows make nests there. They lay their eggs and raise
their young, singing their songs in the place where we worship.
GOD of the Angel Armies! King! God!*

PSALM 84:3 THE MESSAGE

All over the earth, you can see the artistry of God. Mountains reach up toward the sky, majestically pointing toward their Creator—their snow-capped peaks offering silent praise. Farmers' fields of grain wave to the King of Kings. All the earth grows tall, as if reaching up to receive His touch. Animals of every kind show gratitude to their Maker. Birds sing, fireflies dance, and little furry creatures scurry in a fast festivity of life.

God created nature for His glory, and when you look, you can see a glimpse of His greatness. It is a reflection of an even greater glory—that of His presence in the life of a human being like you.

Nature is but a name for an effect whose cause is God.

WILLIAM COWPER

YOUR DAILY REFLECTIONS

_____

_____

_____

_____

*God is faithful; by him you were called into
the fellowship of his Son, Jesus Christ our Lord.*

1 CORINTHIANS 1:9 NRSV

It's a wonderful blessing to have a faithful friend—someone who is there to see you through good times and bad times, when it's convenient and when it isn't. A friend who never leaves your side, whose love is strong and constant, who is always ready to listen, provide wise counsel, and defend you. Do you have a friend like that? You may not know it, but you do.

God wants to be your faithful friend. And unlike earthly friends, He is armed with more than good intentions. God will never fail you. He will be by your side no matter where you are or what you are doing. Open your heart to the most faithful friend you will ever know.

Though men are false, God is faithful.

MATTHEW HENRY

YOUR DAILY REFLECTIONS

_____

_____

_____

_____

Using the Scriptures, the person who serves God
will be ready and will have everything he needs
to do every good work.

2 TIMOTHY 3:17 NCV

The Bible is an amazing book. It is, by many accounts, the greatest collection of literature, history, prophecy, and principles for daily living ever compiled. But the Holy Scriptures can do more than teach you how to live; they can literally put you in touch with the Giver of Life.

The Bible chronicles God's intervention with the human race. It reveals His role as Creator, Redeemer, and Coming King. It describes Him as Friend, Advisor, Comforter, and Guide. And it tells you everything you will ever need to know about how to enter into a relationship with Him.

If you've always wanted to know God, open your Bible and begin to read. You're sure to find Him there.

When you read God's word, you must constantly be saying to yourself, "It is talking to me and about me."

SØREN KIERKEGAARD

YOUR DAILY REFLECTIONS

_____

_____

_____

_____

Beloved, let us love one another, for love is from God;
and everyone who loves is born of God and knows God.

1 JOHN 4:7 NASB

Jesus set an example of love that surpasses any the world had ever known. It was and is an inclusive love that has been poured out equally on the most godly saint and the most despicable sinner. It knows nothing of social status—turning a blind eye to wealth, fame, and fortune. It is color blind, looking past the outward appearance to the heart.

God has called you to love others in the same way He loves you. That may seem impossible, but you can do it if you are willing to open yourself as a channel, letting God's love flow through you to others.

Ask God to help you love others as He loves you. Be part of the greatest circle of love in the universe.

Love seeks one thing only: the good of the one loved.

THOMAS MERTON

YOUR DAILY REFLECTIONS

_____

_____

_____

_____

He that findeth his life shall lose it:
and he that loseth his life for my sake shall find it.

MATTHEW 10:39 KJV

Do you ever wonder about the meaning of life? Why are you here? What it's all about? If you do, you aren't alone. Most people ponder these questions. And God is available to help you find the answers.

Inviting God into your life opens all the doors of discovery. As you get to know Him and learn to listen to His voice, you will receive insight into the reason why God created you. He will reveal His plan and purpose for your life.

Why stand around wondering when you can have the answers to your questions? God is eager to guide you as you open the Scriptures and read about His plans and purposes. Give Him an opportunity to fill you in.

Let God have your life;
he can do more with it than you can.

DWIGHT LYMAN MOODY

YOUR DAILY REFLECTIONS

_____

_____

_____

_____

Be strong and of a good courage; be not afraid,
neither be thou dismayed: for the Lord thy God is with thee
whithersoever thou goest.

JOSHUA 1:9 KJV

If you're a Bible reader, you've probably noticed that it contains many admonitions not to fear, not to be afraid, and to be courageous. That's because this world can be one big, scary place. The list of fears and phobias that plague human beings could stretch around the globe.

Fortunately, along with those admonitions, God gives the key to facing them courageously. "Don't fear, *for I am with you*," He says. When you place yourself in God's care, you are safe—not because there is no danger—but because God is bigger and more powerful than any danger you could face.

Courage is simply the ability to act in the face of fear. God will give you the courage you need as you trust Him.

Fear can keep a man out of danger,
but courage can support him in it.

THOMAS FULLER

YOUR DAILY REFLECTIONS

_____

_____

_____

_____

I will instruct you and teach you in the way you should go;
I will guide you with My eye.

PSALM 32:8

When you were a child, someone most likely held your hand to guide you across the street or to your destination. You're no longer a child, but there is still Someone who wants to help you find your way—that Someone is God.

God can provide you with the guidance you need as you make your way through a complex and confusing world. He is eager to take your hand and walk with you until you reach your destination.

If you feel you are drifting, unable to get your bearings, lost or struggling, call out to God. He will help you discover where you are and where you want to go. He will instruct you through the Scriptures. And He will never leave your side.

Deep in your heart it is not guidance that you want
as much as a guide.

JOHN WHITE

YOUR DAILY REFLECTIONS

_____

_____

_____

_____

Jesus said, "I also say to you that you are Peter,
and upon this rock I will build My church;
and the gates of Hades will not overpower it."

MATTHEW 16:18 NASB

When Jesus referred to the Church, He wasn't talking about a building. He was talking about all the people who would believe His message and gather to worship Him. He wasn't concerned with how they worshiped or where. He wasn't impressed by what they chose to wear or what day or hour they chose to meet. He was only interested in their hearts.

You may or may not attend church regularly. While church is important, God isn't nearly as concerned with that as He is with your relationship with Him. Do you know Him personally? Are you aware of how much He loves you and how much He wants to be a part of your life? Open your heart to Him. It will soon become your favorite place of worship.

The true Church is a living organism, a body,
and believers are joined to it by the quiet working
of the Holy Spirit.

CORNELIUS STAM

YOUR DAILY REFLECTIONS

_____

_____

_____

_____

You have preserved me because I was honest;
you have admitted me forever to your presence.

PSALM 41:12 TLB

Imagine a clear, still lake—so clear that you can see through the water all the way to the bottom. Now see yourself taking a stick, reaching down through the water, and stirring up the muck that rests below. Before your eyes, everything changes. What was clear and still a few moments before is now cloudy and agitated.

Your heart is like that lake. As you speak, act, and live honestly, it remains clear and peaceful. But give way to deceit or color the truth, and your heart becomes muddy and agitated.

Keep the waters of your heart transparent and peaceful before God and man. Cling to the truth. Never let it out of your sight.

I consider the most enviable of all titles,
the character of an honest man.

GEORGE WASHINGTON

YOUR DAILY REFLECTIONS

_____

_____

_____

_____

The Lord's plans will stand forever.
His ideas will last from now on.

PSALM 33:11 NCV

God has promised that you will have a future—a planned path of success, a specific road to follow. You may feel that you've stepped off that path and lost your way, ruining His plans for you. To God it is only a pause. His purpose and plan for your life hasn't changed.

When you feel you've taken a misstep, ask God to forgive you. He's ready and able to help you step back onto the course He's set for you. As much as you desire to move forward in life, He wants to see you succeed even more. Don't let past mistakes rob you of your future. Hope in Him and see your dreams fulfilled.

Lord! We know what we are,
but know not what we may be.

WILLIAM SHAKESPEARE

YOUR DAILY REFLECTIONS

Ye are no more strangers and foreigners,
but fellow citizens with the saints,
and of the household of God.

EPHESIANS 2:19

The Bible says that God created men and women specifically for the purpose of fellowship. And it is for that reason that we all have a deep desire not only to have fellowship with God, but also with each other.

That doesn't mean you must have people around you all the time. It simply means that if you are a healthy, well-adjusted person, you will not shrink from interacting with others. In fact, those interactions will help you keep your bearings in the world around you, rightly perceiving your place in the whole.

Even if you don't consider yourself to be much of a people person, make an effort to reach out to someone. You'll be doing a good thing for yourself.

The virtuous soul that is alone and without a master
is like a lone burning coal;
it will grow colder rather than hotter.

JOHN OF THE CROSS

YOUR DAILY REFLECTIONS

_____

_____

_____

_____

Our only goal is to please God.

2 CORINTHIANS 5:9 NCV

Goals are important. They keep you moving forward, stretching yourself, pursuing new challenges. But God doesn't want you to let your goals take over your life. He knows that if you make them too ambitious, you could find yourself lying helpless on the tracks as the train bears down on you.

Be willing to set preliminary goals—goals you are able to adjust after thoughtful consideration and prayer. And, when appropriate, the input of a trusted friend may be warranted. Always set goals that are balanced with other challenges in your life. Make them measurable and time phased. Set goals for one year at a time. Pursuing goals too far in the future can lead to fatigue and discouragement. Let God help you set goals that will work for you.

The tragedy in life doesn't lie in not reaching your goal.
The tragedy lies in having no goal to reach.

BENJAMIN MAYS

YOUR DAILY REFLECTIONS

_____

_____

_____

_____

Jesus said, "The Helper will teach you everything.
He will cause you to remember all the things I told you.
This Helper is the Holy Spirit whom the Father
will send in my name."

JOHN 14:26 NCV

As the third Person of the Godhead, the Holy Spirit is eternal, omnipresent, just, good, and wise. His mission is to be your "Helper," as you go about life as a redeemed child of God.

Your Helper is constantly by your side, encouraging you, helping you find solutions to problems, comforting you during difficult times, convicting you when you are in danger of getting off track. The Holy Spirit has been called the *paraclete*. In the Greek language, that means one who walks alongside another.

It was never God's intention for you to go it alone. He knew it simply would be too difficult. Open your heart to the Holy Spirit. Let Him help you find your way.

The Holy Spirit has promised to lead us step by step
into the fullness of truth.

LEON JOSEPH SUENENS

YOUR DAILY REFLECTIONS

_____

_____

_____

_____

*This is the confidence (the assurance, the privilege of boldness)
which we have in Him: [we are sure] that if we ask anything
(make any request) according to His will (in agreement
with His own plan), He listens to and hears us.*

1 JOHN 5:14 AMP

God not only created you, but He has also redeemed you and given you instant access to His presence through prayer. You have the opportunity to interact with God just as you would a loving father or a trusted friend. The Bible says that when you speak, He will be listening.

Unfortunately, human traditions have placed countless restrictions on the simple act of prayer. These prescribe how, when, where, and for what purpose prayers should be offered. While the Bible offers models for prayer and admonitions about attitudes in prayer, it seems that all God really expects is that you speak to Him honestly and respectfully.

Tell God what's on your mind. He's waiting to hear from you.

Prayer is conversation with God.

CLEMENT OF ALEXANDRIA

YOUR DAILY REFLECTIONS

_____

_____

_____

_____

*If one has the gift of encouraging others,
he should encourage.*

ROMANS 12:8 NCV

The Book of Acts tells us that the early Christians faced many trials and much suffering. They survived and even flourished, however, because they received encouragement from God and each other. They took time to remind each other that they had something special, something that could never be taken from them— a living, eternal, personal relationship with Almighty God.

You, too, can receive the encouragement that comes from knowing God, and nothing you are experiencing now or will encounter in the future can take it away from you. Let God encourage your heart with words of love and promise. Then, thank Him by reaching out and encouraging someone else with a kind gesture, uplifting word, or warm smile.

One of the highest of human duties
is the duty of encouragement.

WILLIAM BARCLAY

YOUR DAILY REFLECTIONS

_____

_____

_____

_____

Great peace have those who love Your law,
and nothing causes them to stumble.

PSALM 119:165

Does your world sometimes get so loud that you want to cover your ears? Do you find yourself frantically searching for a little peace? Relax! You don't have to look far for it, and you can take it with you wherever you go.

God's peace is like your favorite song playing over and over in your heart. It drowns out confusion, worry, anxiety, and stress. It fills you with a knowing that God has everything under control. God's peace is supernatural calm in the midst of the storm.

When you feel the world swirling around you, focus on God. Let Him turn up the music of His love in your heart until it drowns out the cares of this life.

Peace rules the day when Christ rules the mind.

AUTHOR UNKNOWN

YOUR DAILY REFLECTIONS

_____

_____

_____

_____

Like newborn babies, crave pure spiritual milk,
so that by it you may grow up in your salvation,
now that you have tasted that the Lord is good.

1 Peter 2:2–3 NIV

Children like to measure their height to see how much they've grown. You can measure your spiritual growth by looking into the Scriptures. There you will find the description of godly character and attitudes—love, joy, peace, and patience, to name a few. The more you grow, the more you exhibit those characteristics in your life.

You can encourage spiritual growth in your life by spending time with God. That might mean talking to Him through prayer, singing His praises, or reading the Bible—His words of instruction, encouragement, and inspiration, written just for you.

Make sure you don't neglect your spiritual growth. One day your body will die, but your spirit will live on forever.

If we don't change, we don't grow.
If we don't grow, we are not really living.
Growth demands a temporary surrender of security.

Gail Sheehy

YOUR DAILY REFLECTIONS

_____

_____

_____

_____

Jesus said, "Your heart will always be where your riches are."
MATTHEW 6:21 GNT

The Bible indicates that riches can be a mixed blessing. On the one hand, they relieve the worry and concern about the immediacy of personal needs, but they can also create other problems.

The Bible says: *Give this command to those who are rich with things of this world. Tell them not to be proud. Tell them to hope in God, not their money. Money cannot be trusted, but God takes care of us richly. He gives us everything to enjoy. Tell the rich people to do good and to be rich in doing good deeds. Tell them to be happy to give and ready to share. By doing that, they will be saving a treasure for themselves in heaven* (1 Timothy 6:17–19 NCV).

There is nothing wrong with people possessing riches.
The wrong comes when riches possess people.
BILLY GRAHAM

YOUR DAILY REFLECTIONS

_____

_____

_____

_____

*Clothe yourselves with compassion, kindness,
humility, gentleness and patience.*

COLOSSIANS 3:12 NIV

Do you realize that when you say a kind word or offer a kind gesture, you are imitating God? You are. The Bible says that kindness is a fruit—a by-product—of God's Holy Spirit. It is part of His character. When you treat others with kindness, you are treating them the way God treats you.

Forget the theory that too much kindness can make you appear weak or that acts of kindness should only be offered in response to kindness from others. It pleases God to see kindness flowing freely from your life, without thought of reciprocation. Rather than indicating weakness, it makes you an initiator. That takes strength and courage. So open your heart and establish kindness as part of your character.

Be the living expression of God's kindness:
kindness in your face, kindness in your eyes,
kindness in your smile, kindness in your warm greeting.

MOTHER TERESA

YOUR DAILY REFLECTIONS

_____

_____

_____

_____

As he thinks in his heart, so is he.

PROVERBS 23:7

Do you sometimes feel that your thoughts are carrying on a conversation without you? That probably means your mind is full of cares, worries, and negative thinking. The only way to control your thoughts is to make conscious choices concerning what you think about.

When a negative thought comes your way, try countering it by meditating on how valuable you are to God. Pause to consider His great love for you. Ponder a Bible promise. Count your blessings, recalling the times God has provided for you.

God will not usurp your power over your mind. He has given it to you, along with your free will, to order and control. But He promises to help you deal with your thoughts if you ask Him.

Our best friends and our worst enemies are our thoughts.
A thought can do us more good than a doctor
or a banker or a faithful friend.
It can also do us more harm than a brick.

FRANK CRANE

YOUR DAILY REFLECTIONS

Do not neglect to show hospitality to strangers,
for by this some have entertained angels without knowing it.
HEBREWS 13:2 NASB

Perhaps you know someone who oozes with hospitality—someone quick to accommodate any guest, incredibly polite and cheerful, warm, considerate, cordial, and who loves to entertain. Perhaps you're a person like that—friendly and generous—or perhaps you aren't.

If you draw back from inviting people into your home, it may be time to push forward. Receiving people graciously pleases God. Just as He welcomes you into His heart and will one day invite you into His heavenly home, His desire is for you to open your heart and your home to others. Does that mean He expects you to entertain every night? Of course not. But He does expect you to do it graciously as opportunities come your way. Why not invite someone over today?

When there is room in the heart,
there is room in the house.
DANISH PROVERB

YOUR DAILY REFLECTIONS

_____

_____

_____

_____

*Jesus said, "Come to Me, all you who labor
and are heavy laden, and I will give you rest."*

MATTHEW 11:28

How was your week? Exhausting? You come home after a long week and begin the home projects that are always waiting. If you take time to rest, you may even feel a little guilty, as if you are wasting precious time or being lazy. Perish the thought.

God has actually mandated that one day of your week be set aside for rest. It will be medicine to your active mind and body. But, rest shouldn't be relegated only to that day. It's also wise to take a few minutes in the course of every day to pause and take a breather.

Your Creator rested on the seventh day of creation. If Almighty God took time to rest, shouldn't you?

What is without periods of rest will not endure.

OVID

YOUR DAILY REFLECTIONS

_____

_____

_____

_____

Your faithfulness endures to all generations;
You established the earth, and it abides.

PSALM 119:90

Faithfulness—reliability, dependability, and trustworthiness—is a characteristic so vital that other virtues lose their power without it.

Consider this: You have been volunteering for an organization that provides meals for the elderly. You have committed to be there three times a week. But suppose you have been showing up only once a week or even twice a week. Your good deed has now taken on a negative aspect. The organization and the elderly people it serves are being disadvantaged as a result of your lack of faithfulness.

God wants you to follow His example. He doesn't make promises He doesn't intend to keep. You shouldn't either. He always keeps His word. So should you.

He does most in God's great world
who does his best in his own little world.

THOMAS JEFFERSON

YOUR DAILY REFLECTIONS

_____

_____

_____

_____

Nothing living or dead, angelic or demonic,
today or tomorrow, high or low, thinkable or unthinkable—
absolutely nothing can get between us and God's love.

ROMANS 8:38–39 THE MESSAGE

The very definition of love begins with God, and the very definition of God begins with love. Love is more than His character; it is the essence of His being. And the miracle, the wonder of it, is that God poured out that love, poured out Himself, for you!

Before you ever breathed your first breath, spoke your first word, took your first step, He loved you. Why? Because you are His unique creation, the work of His hands. He made you in His own image, and He loves you as deeply as He loves Jesus.

Don't run from God's love—run to it! He left the decision in your hands when He gave you a free will. Now He waits for you to return His love.

Every existing thing is equally upheld in its existence
by God's creative love.

SIMONE WEIL

YOUR DAILY REFLECTIONS

_____

_____

_____

_____

The LORD is a stronghold for the oppressed,
a stronghold in times of trouble.

PSALM 9:9 NRSV

Simple pleasures such as chocolate, a balloon bouquet, or a card may bring you a moment of comfort during a difficult time; but the comfort God gives can do so much more. It can provide a soothing balm for your nerves, free you from fear and anxiety, and fill you with hope and assurance.

Like a loving earthly father, God's heart aches to ease your pain and lift your spirit. But He will never crowd you. He'll wait patiently for the day that you call on Him. Lift your face up to the heavens and ask God for His comforting touch. Let it cover you like a warm blanket and penetrate to the deepest reaches of your soul.

It will greatly comfort you if you can see
God's hand in both your losses and your crosses.

CHARLES HADDON SPURGEON

YOUR DAILY REFLECTIONS

_____

_____

_____

_____

Be humble and give more honor to others than to yourselves.
PHILIPPIANS 2:3 NCV

Exercising humility means that you are willing to waive your rights and take a lower place than might be your due. It does not require you to underrate yourself, but to live with an appropriate understanding of who you are. It is not a sign of weakness, but rather the hallmark of a healthy self-esteem.

Jesus humbled Himself when He agreed to be the sacrifice for our sins. The crown Prince of Heaven, the Holy Son of God allowed Himself to be beaten and crucified to pay the penalty for our sin. Because He knew exactly who He was, He could choose to humble Himself on our behalf.

Embrace humility, just as Jesus did, so that you might accomplish God's special mission for your life.

If you are humble, nothing will touch you,
neither praise nor disgrace,
because you know what you are.
MOTHER TERESA

YOUR DAILY REFLECTIONS

_____

_____

_____

_____

Jesus said, Thou shalt love the Lord thy God with all thy heart, and with all thy soul, and with all thy mind, and with all thy strength: this is the first commandment. And the second is like it, namely this, Thou shalt love thy neighbour as thyself.
MARK 12:30–31 KJV

I n the Bible, Jesus established a pattern for your priorities. He said that you are to first love the Lord your God with all your heart, soul, mind, and strength and then love your neighbor as yourself.

God is relational. He always puts others first. And that's what He's instructed us to do in this statement. Your relationship with God must come first because He is the wellspring—the source—of all that you need.

God says your second priority should be yourself. Does that surprise you? Until you are strong and healthy, fully established in God's love, you have little to offer anyone else.

Your last priority is to those who are nearby. This would include your family, your friends, and of course, the folks next door.

The main thing is to keep the main thing the main thing!
AUTHOR UNKNOWN

YOUR DAILY REFLECTIONS

The LORD longs to be gracious to you, and therefore
He waits on high to have compassion on you.

ISAIAH 30:18 NASB

The Bible recounts many examples of God's kindness and compassion. He heard the cries of the Israelites as they suffered as slaves in Egypt and set them free. He responded to the grave situation of a poor widow woman by providing her with oil and meal in a time of famine. He sent His Son to redeem your life.

God doesn't change. He is just as compassionate today as He was back in Bible times. When you call out to Him, He will hear you and set in place a plan to rescue you, to comfort you, to provide for you.

God loves you. He wants to help you deal with the issues in your life. Lift your voice to Him, knowing that He will hear and pour out His compassion on you.

Man may dismiss compassion from his heart,
but God will never.

WILLIAM COWPER

YOUR DAILY REFLECTIONS

_____

_____

_____

_____

Be patient when trouble comes. Pray at all times.

If it were not for God's patience with us, who knows how many times He would have wiped the slate clean and begun again. But God never gives up. He waits and hopes and gently woos. Then He patiently waits again for growth and maturity.

If God can find it in His heart to be patient, shouldn't you follow His example? When you feel frustrated and out of patience with someone—a spouse, a friend, a coworker, a neighbor, a child, a parent—rather than choosing to give up, hang on! Ask God to extend your patience in supernatural ways—to others and to yourself. Patience doesn't make you a patsy; it makes you more like God.

Be patient with everyone, but above all, with yourself.

SAINT FRANCIS DE SALES

YOUR DAILY REFLECTIONS

_____

_____

_____

_____

He shall strengthen your heart, all you who hope in the LORD.
PSALM 31:24

Hope is a wish or desire accompanied by confident expectation of its fulfillment. You carry many hopes—earnest expectations—for your future, your family, your career, and your health. It's a mistake, though, to place your hope in people and things that will sooner or later fail you—a good job to fulfill your hope of financial prosperity, someone you hope will be a true and faithful friend. Circumstances change and people disappoint—that's life.

But God will never fail you. He is the only One who can be trusted to sustain your hope, because His power transcends circumstances and the good intentions of human beings. When you place your hope in Him, you will not be disappointed.

What oxygen is to the lungs, such is hope
for the meaning of life.
HEINRICH EMIL BRUNNER

YOUR DAILY REFLECTIONS

_____

_____

_____

Be gentle with one another, sensitive. Forgive one another as quickly and thoroughly as God in Christ forgave you.

EPHESIANS 4:32 THE MESSAGE

The Twenty-third Psalm describes God as a gentle Shepherd who cares lovingly for His sheep. Gentle Shepherd? Does that seem like an unlikely contrast to the way you perceive God—Almighty God, Mighty Warrior, Righteous Judge? Maybe so. But, according to the Bible, gentleness is as much a part of God's character as strength and justice.

It is the gentle part of God that motivates Him to guide and sustain you through difficult times. The Creator of the universe reaches down to comfort you in times of sorrow. It seems that God does not feel that gentleness compromises His strength at all—in fact, it fortifies it.

Free yourself from the idea that showing gentleness makes you appear weak. It just isn't true. God has always known that, and now you know it too.

Nothing is so strong as gentleness,
nothing so gentle as real strength.

SAINT FRANCIS DE SALES

YOUR DAILY REFLECTIONS

_____

_____

_____

_____

*I know whom I have believed and I am convinced that He
is able to guard what I have entrusted to Him until that day.*
                                        2 TIMOTHY 1:12 NASB

God never gives up! It took determination to create the earth and all that it contains. And He was determined when He created you—determined that you would become all He has created you to be.

He will never bully you nor usurp the free will He has given you. But with determination, He will continue to love and care for you, waiting patiently for the day when you acknowledge His hand on your life and choose to love Him in return. He believes in you and in all you have the potential to become.

Seek Him and His wonderful plan for your life. The two of you will make a great team—united in your determination to fulfill your destiny.

Become a mountain climber on the cliffs of
God's majesty, and let the truth begin to overwhelm you
so that you will never exhaust the heights of God.
                                        JOHN PIPER

YOUR DAILY REFLECTIONS

_____

_____

_____

_____

> *How great is your goodness,*
> *which you have stored up for those who fear you.*
>
> PSALM 31:19 NIV

Goodness is a moral condition—a deliberate preference for what is right and persistence to choose and follow it. Does that sound like a standard too high for you to aspire to?

The truth is that pure goodness is an impossible dream for any human being to undertake. Fortunately, you don't have to depend on your own resources to obtain goodness. God has made a way.

First, God has wrapped you in His goodness and declared you to be "good," simply because you are His child. Then, as you spend time with Him, His goodness will literally begin to rub off on you. Slowly but surely, God will teach you to walk in His example—consistently, deliberately, persistently choosing the good and following it.

> God's goodness is the root of all goodness;
> and our goodness, if we have any,
> springs out of his goodness
>
> WILLIAM TYNDALE

YOUR DAILY REFLECTIONS

_____

_____

_____

_____

We will shout for joy when you succeed.
We will raise a flag in the name of our God.

PSALM 20:5 NCV

Would it surprise you to know that God is committed to your success? Like a loving Father, He desires to see you become all you are destined to be. He wants to help you develop your gifts, grow in character, and live a happy, fulfilled life.

God also wants to make sure that you don't get caught up in misleading, temporal measures of success and miss out on those things that truly matter—the things that may seem ordinary and mundane, but in reality are the good and satisfying things in life. He wants to see you succeed in your marriage and with your children. He wants to see you sustain long, rewarding friendships and thrive in your relationship with Him.

Set your sights on becoming a success—God's way.

What a tragedy to climb the ladder of success,
only to discover that the ladder
was leaning against the wrong wall.

ERWIN W. LUTZER

YOUR DAILY REFLECTIONS

_____

_____

_____

_____

*The grace (blessing and favor) of the Lord Jesus Christ
(the Messiah) be with your spirit.*

PHILEMON 1:25 AMP

Grace is free and unmerited favor. You don't have to do anything to receive it. When someone performs an act of goodwill toward another for no reason other than to show kindness, you know grace is at work. Grace doesn't expect payment—it's a gift given with no strings attached.

God's grace was extended to you when He looked down from Heaven and chose to make you His child. He took upon Himself the price you owed—the price exacted by sin and your poor choices and selfish behaviors.

Receive God's grace today. It is a gift, extended to you without thought of reciprocation. All you need do is reach out and take His hand. As you do, your life will be transformed.

There is nothing but God's grace. We walk upon it;
we breathe it; we live and die by it;
it makes the nails and axles of the universe.

ROBERT LOUIS STEVENSON

YOUR DAILY REFLECTIONS

_____

_____

_____

_____

A wise man's heart discerns both time and judgment.

ECCLESIASTES 8:5

What if you knew exactly how much time—how many years, days, hours—you would have here on Earth? Would you make any changes in the way you live your life? It's a question worth considering.

Of course, only God knows how many days your life will contain. And although He most likely isn't going to reveal that information to you, He has given some good advice in the Scriptures. He admonishes you to be a good steward of time, to use it wisely, sober-mindedly. And you aren't to assume that you will be here even one more day—for no one knows what lies ahead. The bottom line is, entrust yourself to God and let Him help you make every minute count.

Time is not a commodity that can be stored for future use.
It must be invested hour by hour.

THOMAS EDISON

YOUR DAILY REFLECTIONS

_____

_____

_____

_____

If we have food and clothing, we will be content with that.
1 TIMOTHY 6:8 NIV

Contentment is simply being satisfied with what you have and who you are—not so easy in a world where everyone seems to be grasping for all they can get. The inner drive you feel to better yourself is God-given. It motivates you to grow in all the aspects of your life. But if that drive becomes unbalanced, it spawns insecurity and the sense that others are passing you by. If it goes unchecked, soon you will feel compelled to get ahead at all costs.

God doesn't want you always striving any more than He wants you always standing still. What He does want is for you to be satisfied—content—with who you are and what you have at any given time in your life. If you are having difficulty getting there, God can help.

God is most glorified in us when
we are most satisfied in him.

JOHN PIPER

YOUR DAILY REFLECTIONS

_____

_____

_____

_____

All the angels are spirits who serve God and are sent to help those who will receive salvation.

HEBREWS 1:14 NCV

The Bible says that angels exist and that they are here to care for those who will receive salvation. They are God's emissaries between Heaven and Earth.

But there are some things you should understand about the ministry of angels. They are not the creatures typically described in folklore and popular art. The Bible says that there are certain ways to identify an angel sent from God.

First, God's angels don't draw attention to themselves. Glorifying God and carrying out His instructions are an angel's only concerns. In addition, the actions of God's angels never contradict the Holy Scriptures or move contrary to God's character.

Thank God for the angels that move invisibly in and out of your life. One day, you might even spot one doing God's bidding.

Millions of spiritual creatures walk the earth unseen, both when we sleep and when we awake.

JOHN MILTON

YOUR DAILY REFLECTIONS

_____

_____

_____

_____

A generous person will be enriched.

PROVERBS 11:25 NRSV

Have you ever given any thought to what the world would be like if God were a tight-fisted miser? It's impossible to imagine the mountains without snow-capped peaks, trees without branches full of blossoms, children without innocence and laughter, life without redemption. God has been indescribably generous with us, and all He asks in return is that we follow His example by being generous with one another.

The next time you reach out to help someone, make it a generous offering—more than is required, more than would be expected. Instead of giving only what you no longer want or need, give of your best, your finest. Open your arms and your heart, and give generously—like God.

He who gives what he would as readily throw away,
gives without generosity; for the essence
of generosity is in self-sacrifice.

SIR HENRY TAYLOR

YOUR DAILY REFLECTIONS

_____

_____

_____

_____

The LORD will guide you always; he will satisfy your needs
in a sun-scorched land and will strengthen your frame.

ISAIAH 58:11 NIV

The Bible says that God has made a firm commitment to provide for those who place themselves in His care. That doesn't mean that He's passing out free lunches. He still expects you to work diligently and responsibly so that you will have enough for yourself and even some left over to share with others.

In every life, however, there are times of need. That need could be financial, but it could just as easily be emotional, physical, or even spiritual. No matter what it is that you lack, God is faithful, and He will provide what you need.

The next time you find yourself deficient in an area, don't try to go it alone. Call on God and expect to see His provision.

Where God guides, He provides.

AUTHOR UNKNOWN

YOUR DAILY REFLECTIONS

_____

_____

_____

_____

The LORD is the strength of my life.

PSALM 27:1

Can you remember a time when you felt so weak, so exhausted that you were sure you couldn't go on? Perhaps it was the result of a physical illness, the death of a loved one, or a time of extraordinary mental stress.

You should know that in those difficult times, God has promised to undergird you with His divine strength. That provision is available to you whenever you need it. All you have to do is ask.

You don't have to wait until your heart becomes overwhelmed to call on Him. He is waiting to hold you up and fill you with inner strength—during bad times and even during good times. Just call on Him!

When God is our strength, it is strength indeed;
when our strength is our own, it is only weakness.

SAINT AUGUSTINE OF HIPPO

YOUR DAILY REFLECTIONS

_____

_____

_____

_____

Shout to the LORD, all the earth;
break out in praise and sing for joy!

PSALM 98:4 NLT

Birds sing, tree branches dance in the wind, and God gave you a voice to sing praise to Him. Maybe you don't feel your voice warrants a microphone and stage, but to God's ears, there is no lovelier sound. It ushers you into His presence.

Your praise doesn't need to be limited to singing either. Shout to the Lord with thanksgiving. Praise Him for the wondrous works of His hands in your life. Dance and jump and clap and, on occasion, sit quietly and worshipfully in His presence.

God is eager to receive your praise, no matter how you choose to give it. Like a loving father glowing in the warmth of his children's adulations, God cherishes the praises of His children.

There is nothing that pleases God so much as praise.

AUTHOR UNKNOWN

YOUR DAILY REFLECTIONS

_____

_____

_____

_____

God's love has been poured into our hearts through
the Holy Spirit that has been given to us.

ROMANS 5:5 NRSV

The Scriptures say that God is love. He is the essence of it, the fulfillment of it, the source of it. And when you come to know Him, you are the recipient of that great and boundless ocean of love.

Never again will you feel that no one cares for you. Your Creator cares. Never again will you wonder if His love for you will end. God has promised that nothing—absolutely nothing—can separate you from His love. Never again will you ask yourself if your life has value. As the object of God's unlimited love, you are of great value.

Carry that love with you as you walk through your world each day, and give those with whom you come into contact a sample of what real love—God's love—is all about.

Jesus did not come to make God's love possible,
but to make God's love visible.

AUTHOR UNKNOWN

YOUR DAILY REFLECTIONS

_____

_____

_____

_____

My God will fully satisfy every need of yours
according to his riches in glory in Christ Jesus.

PHILIPPIANS 4:19 NRSV

Did you choose your profession with the idea of getting rich? If not, you may be one of those people who has answered a higher calling. But that initial desire to do something important with your life, something that requires sacrifice and commitment, may become buried under a mountain of anxiety about bills and making ends meet. It may cause you to resent those you've dedicated your life to help.

If you are staying the course, you should take courage in the fact that God knows your needs. You can count on Him to provide unique ways to supplement your income and creative ideas for living within your means. He's called you for a purpose, and when you do your part, He will do His.

If a person gets his attitude toward money straight,
it will help straighten out almost every other area
in his life.

BILLY GRAHAM

YOUR DAILY REFLECTIONS

_____

_____

_____

_____

The LORD gives wisdom;
from his mouth come knowledge and understanding.

PROVERBS 2:6 NRSV

Do you ever face challenges that don't seem to improve, despite your best efforts? Perhaps there is a problem with your child, a friend, or someone at work. At times, it may seem as if you have no answers. How can you break through in such a situation?

Pray for wisdom as you search for ways to set things right. God knows the specifics of the problem and the needs of those involved, and He can help you find an angle when no one else can.

God has gifted you with the talents and skills you need to do the job He's called you to do. Turn to Him often for wisdom and insight.

Wisdom is a gift direct from God.

BOB JONES

YOUR DAILY REFLECTIONS

_____

_____

_____

_____

Forgetting what lies behind and straining forward
to what lies ahead, I press on toward the goal for
the prize of the heavenly call of God in Christ Jesus.

PHILIPPIANS 3:13–14 NRSV

Setting goals is an important part of becoming successful. You must know what you want to do and have a plan for how to do it. There are many things to consider when setting goals, and appropriate priorities should top the list. You must take into consideration how your goals may affect your family and others in your life, as well as how they will affect your relationship with God.

In the frenetic pace of the world today, it's easy to forget the most important goal of all—growing closer to God. You will need His wisdom, His counsel, His inspiration, and so much more as you strive to attain your goals. As you get to know Him and His values and priorities, you will sense a renewed purpose and inspiration for what you want to accomplish.

First build a proper goal. That proper goal
will make it easy, almost automatic, to build a proper you.

JOHANN WOLFGANG VON GOETHE

YOUR DAILY REFLECTIONS

He will yet fill your mouth with laughter.

JOB 8:21 NASB

How often do you treat yourself to a good, old-fashioned belly laugh? Admittedly, life can bring pain and seemingly overwhelming responsibility, but it also provides plenty of material for potential laughs. And those laughs are good for you *and* the people around you.

It's easy to become focused on the cares of this world: the threat of terrorism, economic instability, and crime. These are legitimate concerns that require some thought and preparation. But that doesn't mean you should lose your joy for living and go around grim-faced and somber.

And consider this notable bonus: humor strengthens your immune system, making you more resistant to disease—never a bad idea with all those germs floating around you every day.

Laughter adds richness, texture, and color
to otherwise ordinary days. It is a gift,
a choice, a discipline, and an art.

TIM HANSEL

YOUR DAILY REFLECTIONS

_____

_____

_____

_____

*Neither the one who plants nor the one who waters
is anything, but only God who gives the growth.*
                                    1 CORINTHIANS 3:7 NRSV

When you were a child or a young adult, someone planted a seed in you—a desire to grow, learn, and prepare for your future. That seed of promise was watered by teachers, mentors, family, friends, and by your own dreams.

As an adult, you have many opportunities to become the "farmer," planting seeds for future harvests in the lives of others. For example, if you are a parent, you are now planting—or have planted—seeds of knowledge and hope in your children. After planting, the process includes patiently watering and caring for the seed before you see the first signs of growth.

Growth takes time. In fact, it's a process that should never stop. Let God help you continue growing and developing your abilities and be mindful of the opportunities you have to plant or water seeds in others.

Gradual growth in grace, knowledge, faith, love, holiness,
humility, and spiritual-mindedness—all this I see
clearly taught and urged in Scripture.
But sudden, instantaneous leaps from conversion
to consecration, I fail to see in the Bible.
                                    J. C. RYLE

YOUR DAILY REFLECTIONS

_____

_____

_____

Let your speech always be with grace.

COLOSSIANS 4:6 NASB

A childhood saying goes, "Sticks and stones may break my bones, but words will never hurt me." But, words do hurt. They can destroy confidence and self-esteem.

We live in a world of people with diverse backgrounds. Some are fortunate enough to have been raised in homes filled with words of love and encouragement. But there are others who were peppered with hurtful words poisoned with anger.

You may have an opportunity to use what you say to heal and reinforce those who have been exposed to a life of painful words. Those people are all around you. So listen to the words you speak to them. Make sure they are kind and encouraging, filled with grace—God's unmerited favor.

Kind words produce their image on men's souls;
and a beautiful image it is. They smooth,
and quiet, and comfort the hearer.

BLAISE PASCAL

YOUR DAILY REFLECTIONS

_____

_____

_____

_____

*The LORD recompense thy work,
and a full reward be given thee.*

RUTH 2:12 KJV

Have you ever spent untold hours of preparation and work on a worthwhile project and felt that no one knew or cared? Perhaps no one did—no one, that is, but God.

It's sad but true that too few people in today's world take note of the sacrifices that accompany great work these days. But you can be sure that God takes notice of the late hours and "extra miles" that go into doing a great job.

You may not receive the accolades of your peers or others around you, but God will reward you for your labor. Your work matters to Him, and that's ultimately what makes it worth doing.

I long to accomplish a great and noble task;
but it is my chief duty to accomplish small tasks
as if they were great and noble.

HELEN KELLER

YOUR DAILY REFLECTIONS

_____

_____

_____

_____

I will give you a new heart and put a new spirit within you.
EZEKIEL 36:26

Spending all day at your job can be stressful. As the day wears on, you may find yourself snapping at someone rather than taking the time to give a thoughtful response. You may unload on the first family member who crosses your path.

When that happens, God is eager to forgive you and help you forgive yourself so that you can get back to doing the job He's called you to do. He knows that every moment you spend in guilt and recrimination will be a moment lost—a moment that will not be spent influencing the lives of others.

When you know you've blown it, go to God without hesitation. He will help you make it right with the other person and give you a fresh, new start.

I like sunrises, Mondays, and new seasons.
God seems to be saying,
"With me you can always start afresh."

ADA LUM

YOUR DAILY REFLECTIONS

_____

_____

_____

_____

You shall go out in joy, and be led back in peace;
the mountains and the hills before you shall burst into song.

ISAIAH 55:12 NRSV

A re you enduring a season in your life when hope seems hard to find? Like winter in the Snow Belt, you look out the windows of your soul and see nothing but bare branches and wonder whether this season will ever end.

If you're feeling tired and hopeless, find a place where you can enjoy God's nearness and see His awesome greatness in the things He has created. The yellow of the first daffodil, for example, can bring renewed hope that summer is just around the corner.

Maybe it's time to visit the nearest indoor botanical garden or take a walk in the woods where God can renew your soul. You'll be a better person after taking one of these inspirational breaks to enjoy God's gift of nature.

I love to think of nature as an unlimited broadcasting
station through which God speaks to us every hour,
if we will only tune in.

GEORGE WASHINGTON CARVER

YOUR DAILY REFLECTIONS

_____

_____

_____

_____

Whatever you do or say, let it be as a representative
of the Lord Jesus, and come with him into the presence
of God the Father to give him your thanks.

COLOSSIANS 3:17 TLB

In the middle of a difficult day when you're feeling most hard-pressed—that's the time to give God thanks. Perhaps you're at work, dealing with disgruntled coworkers or customers ... or at home, dealing with belligerent children. Instead of giving up in despair, thank God for the opportunity you've been given to exhibit His love. Then take a moment to look into their faces and give thanks for them.

Giving thanks for people who sometimes cause you problems increases your appreciation for each person as God's totally unique creation. It's a reminder that even the difficult people around you have been placed on this earth to fulfill a God-given destiny and are, therefore, precious in His eyes.

No duty is more urgent than that of returning thanks.

SAINT AMBROSE

YOUR DAILY REFLECTIONS

_____

_____

_____

_____

Endurance produces character, and character produces hope.
ROMANS 5:4 NRSV

It seems that in today's busy world with all its knowledge and new technology, many people are overlooking the importance of developing good character. In bygone days, it went without saying that neighbors helped neighbors and a man's word was his bond. Children learned good characteristics by the examples set before them in their parents and teachers.

This is still the best way to produce good character. God's plan is for us to be wise and develop positive character traits not only in our own lives but also in the lives of our children and those we influence. Don't make the mistake of thinking this can be accomplished overnight. It takes time and determination, but the end product is priceless.

Character—the sum of those qualities that make
a man a good man and a woman a good woman.
THEODORE ROOSEVELT

YOUR DAILY REFLECTIONS

_____

_____

_____

_____

> *Anxious hearts are very heavy,*
> *but a word of encouragement does wonders!*
>
> PROVERBS 12:25 TLB

Have you ever considered yourself a cheerleader? You are if you've ever been in a position to cheer someone on in a particular endeavor. And, more than likely, you have experienced situations in which you lacked enthusiasm and needed someone to cheer for you.

Think about a football team. Players say that a cheering, enthusiastic crowd can give them that extra burst of energy needed to make a touchdown. Successful teams make it into the final round of play because of their motivation. Their coaches, as well as enthusiastic fans spurred on by the cheerleaders, encourage them to excel.

Everyone needs a cheerleader, and you have one—God! He created you, understands your potential, and is always nearby cheering you on to victory. All you have to do is tune in.

> The really great man is the man
> who makes every man feel great.
>
> G. K. CHESTERTON

YOUR DAILY REFLECTIONS

_____

_____

_____

_____

A gentle answer turns away wrath.

PROVERBS 15:1 NIV

Gentleness and greatness seem worlds apart, and yet most people who have achieved lasting greatness have been people with gentle hearts. Gentleness does not equal weakness. It equals strength.

Dr. Martin Luther King, Jr. and Mother Teresa achieved greatness not because of strident words, but because of their gentle spirits. They were people of faith who believed in a God of mercy and grace—a God who loves all people, regardless of their color or circumstances.

When your family, friends, and coworkers think about the time they have spent with you, will they remember you as a person who influenced them by your gentle spirit? The Bible says that such people are pleasing to God.

Instead of losing, the gentle gain.
Instead of being ripped off and taken advantage of,
they come out ahead!

CHARLES R. SWINDOLL

YOUR DAILY REFLECTIONS

_____

_____

_____

_____

Do you not know that those who run in a race all run,
but only one receives the prize?
Run in such a way that you may win.

1 CORINTHIANS 9:24 NASB

Runners call it "hitting the wall." In a long endurance race, the body reaches the end of its limits and every muscle and fiber screams to quit. Experienced athletes know that you can push through the barrier and gain a second wind to win.

Living the Christian life is a marathon, and like long-distance runners, most Christians "hit the wall" at some point. But when God called you to this higher purpose, He knew it would take determination to stay the course.

When you feel yourself tiring, becoming discouraged, losing steam, read the Scriptures to regain your sense of mission and bolster your determination. Then look to God to give you a second wind to finish your race.

The difference between the impossible
and the possible lies in a person's determination.

TOMMY LASORDA

YOUR DAILY REFLECTIONS

_____

_____

_____

_____

*You have let me experience the joys of life and
the exquisite pleasures of your own eternal presence.*

PSALM 16:11 TLB

Does it seem like work and family responsibilities have caused you to lose the joy of living that you once had?

Take your eyes off your problems and your "To-Do" list for a few minutes and lift them up to God. When you rest in His presence and meditate on all the good things He's placed in your life, you will begin to experience His joy—a joy that comes from within and is not extinguished by external pressures. Soon you will feel your weariness melting away.

Oh, the "To-Do" list will still have to be dealt with. It won't change—but you will. God's joy will provide a sense of renewed enthusiasm as you undertake the tasks before you.

Life need not be easy to be joyful.
Joy is not the absence of trouble
but the presence of Christ.

WILLIAM VAN DER HOVEN

YOUR DAILY REFLECTIONS

_____

_____

_____

_____

My voice shalt thou hear in the morning, O LORD;
in the morning will I direct my prayer unto thee,
and will look up.

PSALM 5:3 KJV

An old adage says that a day hemmed in prayer is less likely to unravel. That's true. Think back to days when things didn't go as planned. Perhaps you started out in the morning weighted down with your own troubles and then had to deal with a troubling circumstance with a family member or coworker. As you rushed to work or an appointment, you were faced with traffic snarls and delays. By noon, you may have been wondering if you could make it through the day.

A time of prayer each morning—unloading your cares on God and drawing upon His unlimited resources of wisdom and joy—can significantly lighten your load and give you a lift. It's the edge that you need before you face your day.

Prayer should be the key of the day
and the lock of the night.

THOMAS FULLER

YOUR DAILY REFLECTIONS

_____

_____

_____

_____

Beloved, I pray that all may go well with you
and that you may be in good health,
just as it is well with your soul.

3 JOHN 2 NRSV

Staying healthy in body and mind is a challenging proposition these days. In our fast-paced world, it can be difficult to find the time to do all the things that are required to maintain good health.

We all know the basic requirements: wash your hands often, eat a balanced diet, get enough rest and exercise, and control stress so your immune system works at its optimum. But your health is also affected by the condition of your soul. When you are spiritually strong, you have a natural joy that boosts your immune system and helps to ward off infection.

Prayer is an essential aid to good health, so make sure it is high on your priority list. The results will be well worth the effort.

Our prayers should be for a sound mind in a healthy body.

JUVENAL

YOUR DAILY REFLECTIONS

_____

_____

_____

_____

*Jesus said, "Take my yoke upon you and learn from Me,
for I am gentle and lowly in heart, and you will find rest
for your souls. For My yoke is easy and My burden is light."*
MATTHEW 11:29–30

Are you getting adequate rest amidst the busyness of your life, or are you working relentlessly from early morning into the evening? Are weekends spent doing endless chores and taking care of the lawn?

God built rest into His creation plan. Throughout the Scriptures, He talks about the need to rest from your labors. He even set the seventh day aside and designated it as a day of rest. He knew the limitations of the human body, mind, and spirit.

So, be sure to get enough rest in each area. Get a full eight hours of sleep each night for your body, indulge in hobbies to rest your mind, and spend time with God to rejuvenate and renew your spirit.

Life lived amidst tension and busyness needs leisure—
leisure that re-creates and renews.
NEIL C. STRAIT

YOUR DAILY REFLECTIONS

_____

_____

_____

_____

> *I love them that love me;*
> *and those that seek me early shall find me.*
>
> PROVERBS 8:17 KJV

If you are a Christian, you have the awesome privilege and responsibility of sharing God's love with those around you. Many people grew up in homes where strife and instability created an emotional vacuum, and they long to know that they are loved.

You can minister to them through your caring, loving spirit, and you can provide the reassuring voice that they need to hear. Indeed, it is the most important thing that God has called you to do.

God's love is not to be hoarded for yourself alone—He wants it to flow through you into the lives of others. As you give it away, you will discover that your love supply never decreases but continually grows larger.

He who is filled with love is filled with God himself.

SAINT AUGUSTINE OF HIPPO

YOUR DAILY REFLECTIONS

_____

_____

_____

_____

*Go in peace. We have promised by the Lord
that we will be friends.*

1 SAMUEL 20:42 NCV

You may have an acquaintance at work or in your neighborhood with whom you would like to develop a deeper relationship but have not because of shyness. Maybe you just haven't known how to go about it. God is able to help. But be warned, that may mean stepping out of your comfort zone.

Pray for that person specifically for at least a week and ask God to provide an opportunity for you to spend a few minutes together. Rather than focusing on yourself, use the encounter to find out more about the other person. You may be surprised to find that the other person is as eager as you are to strike up a friendship.

You can never establish a personal relationship
without opening up your own heart.

PAUL TOURNIER

YOUR DAILY REFLECTIONS

_____

_____

_____

_____

With righteousness he will judge the needy,
with justice he will give decisions for the poor of the earth.

ISAIAH 11:4 NIV

America is great because it is a nation built on the rule of law. The Constitution defines a system of justice to punish and defend its citizens when those laws are broken. So, why is there so much injustice right here in our nation and even more throughout the world?

It's because, despite their greatness, America and its Constitution are far from perfect. Only God can provide perfect law and true justice. While it may not seem that God's justice is swift, it is sure. It is based on an eternal timetable.

When you see injustice, speak up, do what you can. And when you don't see justice rendered here on Earth, rest in the assurance that God will one day set all things right.

Justice is truth in action.

JOSEPH JOUBERT

YOUR DAILY REFLECTIONS

_____

_____

_____

_____

*The goal of our instruction is love from a pure heart
and a good conscience and a sincere faith.*

1 TIMOTHY 1:5 NASB

Your life is filled with endless possibilities, so you set priorities and vow that those things will be the most important in your life. But priorities are sometimes forgotten as the tyranny of the urgent or the lure of the moment takes over.

Take a minute to reflect on your priorities: God, your family, your friends, and your coworkers, for example. Did you make them your first concern because they clamored for attention? God's priorities always put people and their highest good first. And that's the criteria you should use as you set your priorities.

Learn to say no to extracurricular activities when they shortchange the people in your life. Extra money, prestige, and power are not worth the risk of losing those you love.

Do not let the good things in life rob you
of the best things.

BUSTER ROTHMAN

YOUR DAILY REFLECTIONS

_____

_____

_____

_____

Convince, rebuke, and encourage,
with the utmost patience in teaching.

2 TIMOTHY 4:2 NRSV

Have you ever prayed, "Lord, give me patience and give it to me now." If so, you aren't alone. Sometimes it takes the patience of Job to deal with certain people in your life.

Patience is a fruit of the Holy Spirit, given to anyone who asks. But just like edible fruit, it doesn't mature overnight. And just like an overripe grape left behind at harvest, it can rot on the vine. It needs to be picked and eaten for its sweetness to be tasted.

The next time you find yourself losing patience with someone, take a deep breath and ask God to help you control your temper, so you can deal with that person in love. Although their behavior may not be appropriate, perhaps you can encourage them with your patience.

Patience is the companion of wisdom.

SAINT AUGUSTINE OF HIPPO

YOUR DAILY REFLECTIONS

_____

_____

_____

_____

To every thing there is a season,
and a time to every purpose under the heaven.

ECCLESIASTES 3:1 KJV

Do you feel like the year is flying by so quickly that there's just not enough time to accomplish all the goals you've set? It's a common problem. Life seems to be full of interruptions, and even good interruptions take up valuable time. But don't let that steal your joy, because there's always enough time in each day to do God's will.

Goals are important, but God measures time through the lens of eternity. The extra time you spend helping others is not lost. Investing in others by giving them your time and attention can be a gratifying experience that will bring great benefits not only to their lives but also to your own.

Use time wisely, but relax and know that God has given you more than enough time to accomplish His purpose for you.

Only eternal values can give meaning to temporal ones.
Time must be the servant of eternity.

ERWIN W. LUTZER

YOUR DAILY REFLECTIONS

_____

_____

_____

_____

Faith is the assurance of things hoped for,
the conviction of things not seen.

HEBREWS 11:1 NASB

Do you ever wonder if your life is making a meaningful difference in the world? Although you love God and strive to be a good example, do you sometimes lose faith in your ability to impact the lives of those in your realm of influence?

Believing without seeing is sometimes difficult, but when you are living according to God's will and being a faithful witness to those around you, you must choose to believe, even if you don't see the desired results.

Today, pray that God will strengthen and renew your faith that others are being positively impacted by your life.

Faith is the final meaning of human existence,
and the answers to the questions on which all our
happiness depends cannot be found in any other way.

THOMAS MERTON

YOUR DAILY REFLECTIONS

_____

_____

_____

_____

The fruit of righteousness is sown in peace
by those who make peace.

JAMES 3:18

Peace can be elusive. People everywhere long for it, work for it, or protest for it. You may be one of those people—desperate to find peace in the midst of your high-anxiety situation.

God says in the Scriptures that peace is only found in Him. It's a direct result of His presence in your life. No matter what's going on around you, you can pause for a moment and focus your thoughts on Him and peace will begin to well up within you.

Practice thinking about God in those brief quiet moments of your busy days. The more you think about Him, the more His peace—a supernatural peace that is beyond your understanding—will permeate your life.

Peace is not the absence of conflict,
but the presence of God no matter what the conflict.

AUTHOR UNKNOWN

YOUR DAILY REFLECTIONS

_____

_____

_____

_____

If we hope for what we do not see,
we wait for it with patience.

ROMANS 8:25 GNT

Are you going through a difficult time right now? Have you lost hope that circumstances will ever change? Hopelessness can rob you of joy and steal each precious moment.

Biblical hope is more than just expectation or a desire that something wonderful is waiting around the bend. It is a confident trust that God's plans for your life are right and good. When you put your trust in Him, no matter what is happening at the moment, you can look to today and your future with hope because He is there.

God Himself is your hope, in this life and for all eternity. You can confidently step into your future, knowing that God will always be with you—no matter what.

There is no medicine like hope, no incentive so great,
and no tonic so powerful as expectation
of something tomorrow.

SAMUEL JOHNSON

YOUR DAILY REFLECTIONS

_____

_____

_____

_____

Trust in Him at all times, O people;
pour out your heart before him; God is a refuge for us.

PSALM 62:8 NRSV

If you have ever been betrayed, and most everyone has been at one time or another, it might be difficult for you to trust others.

But, there is Someone you can trust completely, Someone who will never betray a confidence, Someone you can be sure is always looking out for your best interests. That Someone is God.

You can tell Him your deepest thoughts and go to Him with your toughest questions. Sometimes His answers might not make sense right away, but trust His wisdom and you will one day see His purpose.

As you learn to trust God, you will find yourself beginning to trust others again as well. Let Him show you how to open your heart.

All I have seen teaches me to trust the Creator
for all I have not seen.

RALPH WALDO EMERSON

YOUR DAILY REFLECTIONS

_____

_____

_____

_____

Some friends play at friendship but a true friend sticks closer than one's nearest kin.

PROVERBS 18:24 NRSV

True friendship is a wonderful treasure that can enhance your life immensely. In a world where peer pressure is a reality of life, friendships can provide confidence and stability. If you have been blessed with good friends, you already know that.

Choosing a friend is an important decision—one that requires careful consideration and much prayer. Choosing the wrong people to be your friends can have devastating consequences, so asking God to help you make good choices is important.

Remember that developing friendships is a two-way street. You must be a good friend if want to have a good friend. And inviting God to be a part of your friendships just makes them stronger.

Be careful of the friends you choose for you
will become like them.

W. CLEMENT STONE

YOUR DAILY REFLECTIONS

_____

_____

_____

_____

The Lord is my strength, my song, and my salvation.
He is my God, and I will praise him.

EXODUS 15:2 TLB

Strength comes in many shapes and sizes. Some people are strong communicators. Some are physically strong. Still others may look small on the outside, but stand tall in their convictions. In what ways are you strong? And, in what ways do you need to be strengthened?

The key to shoring up your weak areas is to draw your strength from God's unlimited resources. You can do that by fortifying yourself through prayer, Bible reading, and practicing the presence of God in your life. The stronger your relationship with God, the stronger and more confident you will feel as you face the world each morning.

As you look to your heavenly Father, you will find that you have all the strength you need and more.

The strength of a man consists in finding out
the way God is going, and going that way.

HENRY WARD BEECHER

YOUR DAILY REFLECTIONS

_____

_____

_____

_____

Let the favor of the Lord our God be upon us;
and confirm for us the work of our hands.

PSALM 90:17 NASB

How do you continue to motivate yourself day after day to do the work that God has given you to do? Working is a marathon, not a sprint, and it takes endurance to succeed.

God has gifted you with special abilities, but He knows that you will never be able to do your job without Him. Instead of depending on your own abilities, depend on His to motivate you.

Today, ask God to inspire you to be the best possible employee, mother, husband, wife, or friend you can be. Then, keep your eyes open for the way He will do it. God may even use the least likely person to encourage you.

Motivation determines what you do.
Attitude determines how well you do it.

LOU HOLTZ

YOUR DAILY REFLECTIONS

_____

_____

_____

_____

Let integrity and uprightness preserve me; for I wait on thee.
PSALM 25:21 KJV

When you decide to walk in integrity, you may find yourself facing opposition. But there are worse things in life than being opposed for doing what is right—like the painful edge of a wounded conscience, for example.

No, walking in integrity is not the formula for being popular. But it is the way to please God and garner His favor. So put the opinions of others aside and hold tightly to the path of right thinking, speaking, and living. In the process, your good example is almost certain to positively impact the lives of others—whether you ever know about it or not. Let God's light shine through you today.

There is no such thing as a minor lapse of integrity.
TOM PETERS

YOUR DAILY REFLECTIONS

_____

_____

_____

_____

Do you want to be truly rich?
You already are if you are happy and good.

1 Timothy 6:6 tlb

Many people seem to be pursuing great wealth these days. Maybe you are one of those people. Do you believe that riches can bring you security and happiness? Do you have a deep desire to lead a glamorous lifestyle? If so, you are apt to find, as so many others have before you, that wealth cannot help you become the person God created you to be. But contentment can.

Being content with what God has given you, allows you to look past the distractions and attachments of wealth and possessions and focus on those things—love, faith, hope, godliness—that will bring you security and happiness both in this life and the life to come.

A little is as much as a lot, if it is enough.

Steve Brown

YOUR DAILY REFLECTIONS

_____

_____

_____

_____

Let the wise also hear and gain in learning,
and the discerning acquire skill.

PROVERBS 1:5 NRSV

I'm sure that you've heard the saying, "You never get too old to learn." And it is true. The Scriptures tell us that learning is a lifelong process. No matter how wise or knowledgeable you are, there is always something new to learn. That's what makes life so interesting.

Perhaps you are involved in continuing education courses to stay abreast of the latest information about your field of work. Or you may be taking classes to learn a hobby to enjoy in your leisure time. An unending variety of educational classes are available to enrich your life.

And don't forget the priceless things you can learn from and about God. It's an educational investment that will never stop paying dividends.

In a time of drastic change,
it is the learners who inherit the future.

ERIC HOFFER

YOUR DAILY REFLECTIONS

_____

_____

_____

_____

Grace to you and peace from God our Father,
and the Lord Jesus Christ.

ROMANS 1:7 KJV

You may not always feel God's grace and peace in your life, even though they are always there, available to you in every situation you could possibly face. Too often, those wonderful gifts from God are short-circuited by anxiety, busyness, and self-reliance.

You would think that God would take His beautiful gifts and go home, but He doesn't. He continues to provide them for you, regardless of how you've treated them and Him in the past. So if you find yourself too stressed, too tired, too frustrated to make the most of your day, call on Him. His grace (unmerited favor) and His peace can transform the way you view your day. Then, thank Him for all He's given you—gracefully, of course.

Grace is always given to those ready to give thanks for it.

THOMAS À KEMPIS

YOUR DAILY REFLECTIONS

_____

_____

_____

_____

The LORD is gracious and righteous;
our God is full of compassion.

Do you show compassion for others? Everyone makes mistakes, some silly and some more serious. But God's plan is for you to treat others with the same understanding that you would like to receive when you make a mistake.

People were drawn to Jesus because He had compassion for them. Every word, every action, was filled with His love and desire to see them cared for. In the same way, God wants you to love others and show compassion. Your kindness and concern can bring out the best in them. You may even be responsible for setting someone back on the right path.

Today, ask God to give you a compassionate heart. Learn to empathize with those around you in the same way God empathizes with you.

Anyone can criticize.
It takes a true believer to be compassionate.

ARTHUR H. STAINBACK

YOUR DAILY REFLECTIONS

_____

_____

_____

_____

We have gifts that differ according to the grace given to us.
ROMANS 12:6 NCV

If you have discovered your calling in life and are successfully fulfilling it, you are blessed. There are many today who are still grappling with the questions, "Who am I, and why am I here?"

You may look many places, but you will never find the answers to those questions outside of God. He created you for a purpose and has given you the gifts and talents you need to pursue and fulfill that purpose. Go to Him, humbly and honestly, and ask Him to show you those things He has placed within you and for what purpose He intends them to be used. The revelation of God's gifts in your life may take time, but it's time well spent.

Your talent is God's gift to you.
What you do with it is your gift back to God.
LEO BUSCAGLIA

YOUR DAILY REFLECTIONS

_____

_____

_____

_____

To enjoy your work and to accept your lot in life—
that is indeed a gift from God.

ECCLESIASTES 5:19 TLB

Wealth can be measured in many ways. Some people think of it only in terms of riches and possessions, reflecting a popular bumper sticker that reads, "The one with the most toys wins."

If you are an average person earning midlevel wages (like most of us), you may never live in a mansion or drive expensive luxury cars. But God does not equate wealth with your bank account. Rather, He looks at the abundance of well-being in your heart. If you enjoy your work and thrive on it and have time to enjoy your family and friends, you have true wealth. If you love God and are committed to His will for your life, you have true wealth. How wealthy are you?

God only, and not wealth, maintains the world.

MARTIN LUTHER

YOUR DAILY REFLECTIONS

_____

_____

_____

_____

You should not be like cowering, fearful slaves.
You should behave instead like God's very own children,
adopted into his family—calling him "Father, dear Father."
ROMANS 8:15 NLT

When you think about God, do you see Him as Someone to be feared or do you see Him as a loving, heavenly Father you can approach with confidence? When children feel loved and valued by their parents, they feel free to crawl up into their parents' laps for fun, for comfort, for instruction. You can confidently go to God for the same things and much more.

If you need grace to make it through the day, forget the "thee's" and "thou's" of a formal prayer. Ask God to give you an image of Him with arms open wide. Now crawl up in His lap and soak up His loving presence. He's waiting for you.

The relationship between God and a man
is more private and intimate than
any possible relation between two fellow creatures.
C. S. LEWIS

YOUR DAILY REFLECTIONS

_____

_____

_____

_____

I know the plans I have for you, says the LORD,
plans for your welfare and not for harm,
to give you a future with hope.

JEREMIAH 29:11 NRSV

Today's headlines are enough to leave a person cringing under the covers: crime, terrorism, flesh-eating viruses. The good news is that you don't have to rely on the daily newspaper to determine your outlook on life. You can go directly to the God, the One who holds the world and the future in His hands.

What a relief to know that He is always there, ready and willing to lead you into the future—one manageable step at a time. You can leave the big scary stuff to Him. He's the only one who can do anything about it anyway. So relax. When you see the sun come up in the morning, let it remind you that God has everything under control.

The future is as bright as the promises of God.

ADONIRAM JUDSON

YOUR DAILY REFLECTIONS

_____

_____

_____

_____

As each one has received a gift, minister it to one another,
as good stewards of the manifold grace of God.

1 PETER 4:10 NKJV

When someone sneezes, you say, "God bless you." When you pray over a meal, you say, "Lord, bless this food." When you attend church, your pastor or priest may end the service with a blessing based on Numbers 6: 24, "May the Lord bless you and keep you."

The blessings of God flow out to His children because of His great love. God wants you to pass on His blessings by loving others. Without saying a word, you can bless the people around you with a smile or a look of encouragement.

But, don't forget those spoken blessings. When you have the opportunity, speak words of blessing over the lives of your friends and loved ones. Then watch for and witness the positive impact your words have on them.

Make no mistake about it, responsibilities toward
other human beings are the greatest blessings
God can send us.

DOROTHY DIX

YOUR DAILY REFLECTIONS

_____

_____

_____

_____

Remember now, O LORD, I pray, how I have walked
before You in truth and with a loyal heart,
and have done what is good in Your sight.

ISAIAH 38:3

For some people, loyalty is an outdated concept. Job loyalty has been replaced with moving up in your career. Loyalty in friendship is often overruled by looking out for number one. But God still wants you to be true and committed to those He has placed in your life. After all, He would never push you aside for a better creation.

Times change, that's true. You may work for a huge, impersonal corporation rather than a small business. You may live in a big city, where people are coming and going. But you can still show loyalty by giving 100 percent to your employer and standing by your friends in good times and bad. Character never goes out of style.

Our loyalty is due not to our species but to God.

C. S. LEWIS

YOUR DAILY REFLECTIONS

_____

_____

_____

_____

Jesus said, "Blessed are the merciful:
for they shall obtain mercy.

MATTHEW 5:7 KJV

When Jesus said to be merciful, He was aware that there needed to be retribution for breaking rules. Jesus knew all about repeat offenders. He knew about "tough love" two thousand years before the term was coined.

Still, He exhorts you to be merciful. There are enough times when you need to enforce rules and let people feel the full consequences for their actions. But in the midst of justice, there are times when mercy is more effective.

King David asked, "If you, GOD, kept records on wrongdoings, who would stand a chance? As it turns out, forgiveness is your habit" (Psalm 130:3 THE MESSAGE). Follow God's example and make a habit of being merciful.

He who demands mercy and shows none ruins
the bridge over which he himself is to pass.

THOMAS ADAMS

YOUR DAILY REFLECTIONS

_____

_____

_____

_____

Peace be within your walls, and security within your towers.
PSALM 122:7 NRSV

A re you afraid because of what is happening in the world today? It is understandable to feel some insecurity when things seem to be spiraling into chaos. But if you study history, you will find that every generation has faced similar challenges.

When you feel fearful and insecure, it's a good time to think about the faithfulness of God. When you trust in God, you are assured that no matter what happens, He is with you. He sends His angels to stand guard over you. Even in the midst of chaos, God can bring peace and order to your heart.

You can put the chaotic happenings of the world into proper perspective by reminding yourself of God's promises to be with you and protect you.

Safe am I. Safe am I, in the hollow of His hand.
OLD SUNDAY SCHOOL SONG

YOUR DAILY REFLECTIONS

_____

_____

_____

_____

You, O Lord, are a God merciful and gracious,
slow to anger and abounding in steadfast love and faithfulness.
PSALM 86:15 NRSV

Are you uncertain about God's faithfulness? Do you wonder if He will abandon you in the midst of a difficult situation?

It says in the Bible that God will never leave you, nor will He forsake you. He is always faithful. You can be certain that He will keep His promises to you, because His nature forbids Him to lie. No matter what circumstances you find yourself in, God is right there with you.

When you feel battered on every side by your life, your work, your family, or your friends, call out to God. As certainly as He hears your voice, He will respond by drawing close. You can count on it.

God is faithful, and if we serve him faithfully,
he will provide for our needs.
SAINT RICHARD OF CHICHESTER

YOUR DAILY REFLECTIONS

_____

_____

_____

_____

When my anxious thoughts multiply within me,
Your consolations delight my soul.

PSALM 94:19 NASB

Do you long for peace and rest in your mind and thoughts? Are you plagued with unanswered questions about your life and the lives of those around you? If so, take a deep breath and turn your attention to God.

Scripture says that you should not be anxious, because He knows what you need. When you think about the vastness of God's creation and His great love for you, it will help put your thoughts into proper perspective. In the end, you will see that fear and anxiety—the anticipation of something bad—disallows God's solution. By the time you realize that He's sent the answer, you've already subjected yourself to much mental suffering. Let God fill your mind with His thoughts.

The greatest battles are fought in the mind.

CASEY TREAT

YOUR DAILY REFLECTIONS

_____

_____

_____

_____

Jesus said, "This is the way to have eternal life—
by knowing you, the only true God, and Jesus Christ,
the one you sent to earth!"

JOHN 17:3 TLB

In quiet moments or in the dark of night, you may have thought about where you will spend eternity. Life is finite. There is no way of knowing how long you have on this earth to fulfill God's purpose.

The Old Testament speaks of life as a mere breath. In the New Testament, Jesus spoke many times about the fact that He came to Earth not to condemn the world, but to save it. He died so that He could prepare an everlasting home for you.

Rest assured that if you put your trust in God and His Son Jesus Christ, you have eternal life. Be comforted today in knowing that when you take your last breath in this life, you will take your next in Heaven.

Eternity to the godly is a day that has no sunset.

THOMAS WATSON

YOUR DAILY REFLECTIONS

_____

_____

_____

_____

He that covereth a transgression seeketh love.

PROVERBS 17:9 KJV

A re you holding a grudge against someone? Maybe that person said or did something that you just can't seem to forgive or forget. The incident keeps replaying in your head over and over again.

You may never quite forget it, but God expects you to forgive the one who offended you. He knows that if you harbor anger and unforgiveness, it will eventually destroy you, not the one whom it is directed against. The offender may not even remember the circumstances that have become so important to you. In addition, holding a grudge saps your energy and inspiration. It simply isn't worth it—on any level.

Pray that God will help you to forgive and bring you peace of mind.

Forgiveness is the key that unlocks the door
of resentment and the handcuffs of hate.
It is a power that breaks the chains of bitterness
and the shackles of selfishness.

CORRIE TEN BOOM

YOUR DAILY REFLECTIONS

_____

_____

_____

_____

Jesus said, "I came to give life—life in all its fullness."
                                                    JOHN 10:10 NCV

Are you excited about your life? Do you have a sparkle in your eyes? A spring in your step? When you love doing what God has called you to do, you should feel excitement about what each day will bring.

God gave you life to enjoy in all its richness. It's not even a choice between seeing a glass half empty or half full. God wants you to fill it to the brim with an abundance of His love, joy, and peace. Look for new and interesting ways to do things. Adopt an attitude of adventure.

Most of all, ask God to help you make a change that will result in a renewed sense of wonder about the job you've been called to do. Vow to live with joie de vivre.

Life is either a daring adventure or nothing.
                                                    HELEN KELLER

YOUR DAILY REFLECTIONS

_____

_____

_____

_____

O Lord, we beseech you, give us success!
PSALM 118:25 NRSV

Success can mean many things to many people. For some, it means financial prosperity. For others, it means job satisfaction or successful relationships or a secure future. How do you measure success?

The Bible says that God is the One who can help you find true and lasting success—the kind that doesn't disappear with a financial setback or a bump in your career. The kind that doesn't fade as your good looks diminish and your body ages. Ask God to help you fully understand that success is about "who" you are rather than "what" you do or "what" you have or "how" you look. It is about the imperishable qualities of good character and right thinking. Make sure your success counts.

It is not your business to succeed, but to do right;
when you have done so, the rest lies with God.
C. S. LEWIS

YOUR DAILY REFLECTIONS

_____

_____

_____

_____

*Jesus opened their understanding,
that they might comprehend the Scriptures.*

LUKE 24:45

Theologians, academics, and religious leaders have studied and debated the Scriptures for thousands of years. So how, you may be asking yourself, can you, a regular person, be expected to understand them? It may not be as difficult as you think.

New translations written in simple language abound. If you start with a Bible written for children, it will help you understand the main stories. There are also study Bibles with notes that can put things into perspective for you.

God wants you to seek Him and know Him. That's exactly why the Scriptures were given. Ask Him to enlighten your mind as you read. And, if you feel you need extra clarification and insight, you might try asking a pastor or priest.

When you have read the Bible, you will know it is the word of God, because you will have found the key to your own heart, your own happiness and your duty.

WOODROW WILSON

YOUR DAILY REFLECTIONS

I can do all things through Christ who strengthens me.
PHILIPPIANS 4:13

Do you ever find yourself questioning whether you are strong enough or capable enough to handle the responsibilities that God has placed in your hands?

When you begin to wonder if you're up to the challenge, remember that God has prepared you for what He has given you to do. All through your childhood and young adult years, like a potter with fresh clay on the wheel, He molded and shaped your character, equipping you for what is ahead. He has prepared you in ways you never imagined in order for you to fulfill the purpose He has for your life.

So relax. Whatever God's called you to do, you can do it—and you won't have to do it alone.

When you surrender your will to God,
you discover the resources to do what God requires.
ERWIN W. LUTZER

YOUR DAILY REFLECTIONS

_____

_____

_____

_____

Let the beloved of the LORD rest secure in him,
for he shields him all day long,
and the one the LORD loves rests between his shoulders.

DEUTERONOMY 33:12 NIV

Sometimes life can present so many difficulties that you feel you can't go on one more day. There may be days when you feel as bruised and battle-scarred as a soldier in the field. But, don't despair!

God loves you and He knows that you grow weary. His desire is to comfort you, to take the load off your shoulders, to put His arm around you, and remind you that your diligence and dedication are pleasing to Him.

Open the Bible and read the beautiful words of the Twenty-third Psalm. They were written for you just as they were written for all those who turn to God for comfort. Imagine Him speaking the words directly to you—because He is.

In Christ, the heart of the Father is revealed,
and higher comfort there cannot be than
to rest in the Father's heart.

ANDREW MURRAY

YOUR DAILY REFLECTIONS

_____

_____

_____

_____

That everyone may eat and drink,
nd find satisfaction in all his toil—this is the gift of God.
ECCLESIASTES 3:13 NIV

A re you dissatisfied with your life and the progress you've made toward reaching your goals? Take heart. God didn't place you where you are and put a purpose in your heart in order to make you unhappy or see you fail. He wants you to find joy and satisfaction in what He's called you to do.

Perhaps you are struggling because you're focusing on the wrong things, measuring your progress by the world's standard rather than God's. Step back for a moment. Ask God to show you how He sees things, how He measures your accomplishments. Such an exercise is certain to give you a sense of satisfaction and a fresh perspective.

The world without Christ will not satisfy the soul.
THOMAS BROOKS

YOUR DAILY REFLECTIONS

_____

_____

_____

_____

Jesus said, "In the world you have tribulation,
but take courage; I have overcome the world."

JOHN 16:33 NASB

Have the changes in our economy and other recent world events caused you to feel weak or fainthearted? It takes courage to face the challenges of living in today's world—challenges that have grown more violent and inexplicable in recent years. Just sending your children off to school these days can cause anxiety.

But, all through the Scriptures, God says, "Fear not." He goes before you and sends His angels to watch over you and those you love. There's even a popular bumper sticker that says, "There is nothing that you and God can't handle together."

When you pray, ask God to grant you the courage and the wisdom to deal with any situation that may arise and give you His peace that passes all understanding.

Courage is trusting God!

ANDREA GARNEY

YOUR DAILY REFLECTIONS

_____

_____

_____

_____

Jesus said, "Be ready all the time.
For I, the Messiah, will come when least expected."

LUKE 12:40 TLB

When a woman finds out she is pregnant, she is filled with expectancy. She prepares a nursery and plans for the baby's delivery. Likewise, before walking down the aisle, a bride plans her wedding down to the smallest detail, anticipating the moment when she will look into her bridegroom's eyes and speak her vows.

Are you expectant? The Scriptures promise that Christ will return someday to gather up His own, just like a bridegroom coming for His bride. No one knows exactly when that day will be, but it could be any moment. Are you preparing for His return? Are you waiting expectantly to look into His eyes and see His love for you? Don't hesitate another moment.

The quality of our expectations determines
the quality of our action.

ANDRÉ GODIN

YOUR DAILY REFLECTIONS

_____

_____

_____

_____

Be clothed with humility: for God resisteth the proud,
and giveth grace to the humble.

1 PETER 5:5 KJV

Some think being humble means being weak. But that's simply not the case. True humility is a character trait of God. He has plenty of reason to exalt His accomplishments and remind us of how powerful He is. After all, He created the universe and everything in it. But instead, He focuses on His children—loving, caring for, and encouraging them.

Ask God to help you always exhibit true humility. Go about your business, doing what God has called you to do and remembering that He is your Helper. The Bible says that the day will come when He will exalt you.

It is no great thing to be humble when you
are brought low; but to be humble when you
are praised is a great and rare attainment.

BERNARD OF CLAIRVAUX

YOUR DAILY REFLECTIONS

_____

_____

_____

_____

You will be enriched in every way for your great generosity.
2 CORINTHIANS 9:11 NRSV

The Scriptures point out that it is more blessed to give than to receive and that God rewards a generous heart. Generosity doesn't always come naturally, however. Most of the time it must be taught.

Perhaps you were fortunate enough to grow up in a family where the principles of giving were taught by instruction and example. If so, you have no doubt seen many benefits and blessings as a result.

If these principles are new to you, this might be a good time to try them out. Open your heart and hands to those around you who have needs. The Bible promises that it will come back to you multiplied many times over.

> You do not have to be rich to be generous.
> If he has the spirit of true generosity,
> a pauper can give like a prince.
> CORRINE U. WELLS.

YOUR DAILY REFLECTIONS

_____

_____

_____

_____

Choose life and not death!

2 KINGS 18:32 NIV

Not every choice you make in life will be momentous or have eternal consequences, but every decision contributes to your character. Like a stalactite formed over time by the steady dripping of water, you become the individual you are by your daily actions.

When you use God's standard for making decisions, you will become more like Him with each passing day. You can find out what God's standards are by reading the Scriptures. After all, they were written by God just to help you know and understand Him better.

Put God's Scriptures into your heart, and when you face a tough decision, you will have a powerful resource to help you make it a good one.

Living is a constant process of deciding
what we are going to do.

JOSÉ ORTEGA Y GASSET

YOUR DAILY REFLECTIONS

_____

_____

_____

_____

The mind controlled by the Spirit is life and peace.

ROMANS 8:6 NIV

Physically, you are what you eat, but spiritually, you are what you think. If you worry and stew over a situation, looking for your own answers about how to fix a problem, peace will elude you.

Instead, when something is bothering you, meditate on the nature of God. He has all the answers. Take a moment to think about His greatness. Then, think about what is right in the world, rather than what is wrong with it. Contemplate a scripture, and let its words wash through your mind.

Meditation is about pausing in the midst of your situation and listening to the inner voice of the Holy Spirit. It's like a calm break, designed to give you an opportunity to focus on the One who has the answers.

Let us leave the surface and, without leaving the world, plunge into God.

TEILHARD DE CHARDIN

YOUR DAILY REFLECTIONS

_____

_____

_____

_____

According to thy mercy
remember thou me for thy goodness' sake, O LORD.

PSALM 25:7 KJV

How do you react when another person wrongs you? Is your first reaction to point out the offense and let that person know how unhappy you are? That's a fairly normal tendency, but it certainly isn't the way God wants you to handle such situations.

God is pleased when you are willing to extend goodness and mercy to others. It pleases Him because it is an acknowledgement of the goodness and mercy He has Himself extended to you. It is, in a sense, the equivalent of a "thank you" to God. Let Him know that the goodness He's shown you is appreciated by being good to others—even when they've wronged you.

A Christian should always remember that the value
of his good works is not based on their number
and excellence, but on the love of God
which prompts him to do these things.

JOHN OF THE CROSS

YOUR DAILY REFLECTIONS

_____

_____

_____

_____

Lord, you bless those who do what is right;
you protect them like a soldier's shield.

Are you often afraid? Today's world can be a scary place. It seems as though every day brings news of terrorist attacks, street rioting, or school violence.

But, you must not live your life behind locked doors, either physically or mentally. Instead, trust in God, who promises to provide security to those who call on His name—to make you feel safe even in troubled times. Listen for the quiet, still voice of God alerting you to take shelter in Him when danger is near. Let Him be your armor and shield.

Rest securely in God's protection each day as you continue to do your job and live your life to the fullest.

This is a wise, sane Christian faith: that a man
commit himself, his life, and his hopes to God;
that God undertakes the special protection
of that man; that therefore that man ought
not to be afraid of anything.

GEORGE MACDONALD

YOUR DAILY REFLECTIONS

_____

_____

_____

_____

Patience and encouragement come from God.

ROMANS 15:5 NCV

Does it seem like you spend your days encouraging others, but when you need a lift, no one is there to pat you on the back and say, "Good job"?

When you're feeling discouraged and need someone to reach down and lift you up, spend time with God in prayer. Receive encouragement as you cultivate your relationship with Him, for His Holy Spirit will sustain and validate you when no one else is around. God's very presence will give you the support you need.

The Scriptures are also a source of encouragement that is always available to you. The Book of Psalms is filled with words of grace and promise. Reach out to God. He's waiting to say, "Well done."

Encouragement is oxygen to the soul.

GEORGE M. ADAMS

YOUR DAILY REFLECTIONS

_____

_____

_____

_____

Put on the new man which was created according to God,
in true righteousness and holiness.

EPHESIANS 4:24

In today's high-tech society, identity theft is a common occurrence. By obtaining the right personal information, one person can steal another's name, credit rating, and much more. It's a very real problem.

But, no one can rob you of your identity in Christ. When you seek God and put your trust in Him, He will transform your character and personality, developing within you qualities that no thief can steal. You are one of a kind; you cannot be duplicated.

Today, ask God to show you how to become more like Him. Let your identity come from who you are in Christ rather than from your material possessions, your looks, or what other people say about you.

Is it a small thing in your eyes to be loved by God—
to be the son, the spouse, the love,
the delight of the King of glory?

RICHARD BAXTER

YOUR DAILY REFLECTIONS

_____

_____

_____

_____

You are a God of forgiveness, gracious and compassionate,
slow to anger, and abounding in lovingkindness.

NEHEMIAH 9:17 NASB

Do you feel like God could never forgive you for the things you have done in your life? Be assured there is nothing you could do that God cannot forgive. He sees and knows every one of your thoughts and words and deeds. He saw them before you were born.

That's why He sent His Son Jesus to carry all your sins and misdeeds to the cross, where they would be atoned for once and for all. The payment for your debt was so great that it covers the very worst that human nature can conceive.

Today, receive God's loving forgiveness for your sins and missteps. Let Him wash you white as snow on the inside. Then go and be a better person for Him.

The most marvelous ingredient in the forgiveness
of God is that he also forgets—
the one thing a human being can never do.

OSWALD CHAMBERS

YOUR DAILY REFLECTIONS

_____

_____

_____

_____

The Lord wants honest balances and scales to be used.
He wants all weights to be honest.

PROVERBS 16:11 NCV

Situational ethics have become acceptable in American society. There are those who say that dishonesty in private life does not affect the honesty of public life. The message is that it's okay to do something wrong as long as you don't get caught.

But, God's standards are unchangeable, and all the weights and balances He uses to judge a situation are perfect. Determining to be honest and to tell the truth in every aspect of your life is a goal worthy of pursuing. To encourage your efforts, meditate on the virtues of honesty and the consequences of dishonesty.

God has given you the power to positively influence those around you for good. What an opportunity!

If we be honest with ourselves,
we shall be honest with each other.

GEORGE MACDONALD

YOUR DAILY REFLECTIONS

_____

_____

_____

_____

Suffering produces perseverance;
perseverance, character; and character, hope.

ROMANS 5:3–4 NIV

Children find it difficult to wait for anything. They live in a world of microwave popcorn, instant soup, and cartoons on demand. Yet, as an adult, you know that the enduring things of life seldom come without delay, hard work, and perseverance. Your education took years of study. Your profession involves long hours of concentration and effort. And marriage and raising a family require time, patience, wisdom, and a long-term commitment.

Knowing these things doesn't mean that you always like the waiting and the persevering—like children, you, too, sometimes want to see instant results. But when you feel impatient or frustrated, remember the benefits of perseverance.

Energy and persistence conquer all things.

BENJAMIN FRANKLIN

YOUR DAILY REFLECTIONS

_____

_____

_____

_____

Trust in the LORD and do good;
dwell in the land and cultivate faithfulness.

PSALM 37:3 NASB

After spending time with you, would others describe you as a faithful person? Faithfulness is a trait that must be developed, one faithful act at a time.

For example: You said you'd be at your son's softball game, but you didn't make it. You told your wife you'd be home for dinner, but something came up. You told your boss you'd have that report on his desk by Monday, but you forgot about it. You may think none of these examples are a big deal—but you would be wrong! Every time you fail to keep your commitments, you demonstrate unfaithfulness to those who depend on you.

God is faithful to you. He will never let you down. And He wants you to walk in faithfulness as well.

Faithfulness in little things is a big thing.

SAINT JOHN CHRYSOSTOM

YOUR DAILY REFLECTIONS

_____

_____

_____

_____

I greet you with the grace and peace poured into our lives by
God our Father and our Master, Jesus Christ.

EPHESIANS 1:1 THE MESSAGE

Isn't it refreshing when you pass someone on the street and he or she actually looks up at you and smiles? What about that unexpected act of kindness or word of encouragement?

This is exactly the kind of behavior that God wants you to exhibit. When you treat others with kindness—you are touching them with God's love, you are being His hand extended. You are letting them know you care—and He cares.

It doesn't take much effort to smile and say hello—so don't hold back. You may never know how much your simple gesture means to some lost and lonely soul. But you will know that God is pleased.

Be kind. Remember that everyone you meet
is fighting a hard battle.

HARRY THOMPSON

YOUR DAILY REFLECTIONS

_____

_____

_____

_____

Where there is no counsel, the people fall;
but in the multitude of counselors there is safety.

PROVERBS 11:14

Did you know there are many people who do not realize the benefits of getting good counsel when they are struggling with a particularly difficult problem or decision? They go along for weeks and months at a time, carrying their burden alone, instead of seeking out the counsel of a trusted friend, pastor, or professional counselor.

According to the Scriptures, everyone needs sound guidance. Perhaps you have a personal problem that needs attention or there is a situation at work or with a family member that you don't know how to handle. Are you trying to solve it yourself? God is always available to give you the right answer, but sometimes He may give it to you through another person.

If you're struggling today, pray that God will lead you to wise advisers to help you determine the right course of action.

When we fail to wait prayerfully for God's guidance
and strength, we are saying with our actions,
if not our lips, that we do not need him.

CHARLES HUMMEL

YOUR DAILY REFLECTIONS

_____

_____

_____

*To everything there is a season, a time for every purpose
under heaven: a time to weep, and a time to laugh;
a time to mourn, and a time to dance.*

ECCLESIASTES 3:1, 4

Are you the kind of person who insists on having a little fun every day? You may be thinking, Who me? I have too much to do and too little time to do it! If so, you may be surprised to learn how fun and laughter can help you get it all done.

Look at it this way. Laughter stimulates your breathing and your blood flow. A little spontaneous fun gives your brain and your body a chance to relax their rigid, busy stance and be renewed. Most people find that they go back to work with fresh energy and interest.

Laughter should be a normal part of your daily experience. Try it and you'll be glad you did.

People rarely succeed unless
they have fun in what they are doing.

DALE CARNEGIE

YOUR DAILY REFLECTIONS

_____

_____

_____

_____

The Lord is good to all; he has compassion on all he has made.
PSALM 145:9 NIV

Imagine what it would be like to see the world through God's eyes. How would you feel about the woman in the wheelchair at the grocery store? The neighbor kid who's just found out his folks are getting a divorce? The homeless guy on the park bench?

Seeing individuals the way God does makes you want to put love into action and help. That's compassion kicking in. Compassion doesn't just feel sorry for people. It strives to make a positive difference in their lives. So, ask God to help you see through His eyes—then let you know how you can help. Even if the only action you can take is to pray, your compassion can make a difference in the world.

Man is never nearer the Divine
than in his compassionate moments.
JOSEPH H. HERTZ

YOUR DAILY REFLECTIONS

_____

_____

_____

_____

Where the Spirit of the Lord is, there is freedom.

2 CORINTHIANS 3:17 NIV

Some people believe that relying on God would strip them of their independence and personal freedom. Really—the opposite is true. Relying on God for guidance, strength, comfort, wisdom, and countless other necessities allows you to risk throwing yourself wholeheartedly into the adventure of life.

It's like having a partner belay your rope while you are rock climbing. It gives you the freedom and courage to tackle higher and harder climbs. The same is true with God. The closer the "partnership" you have with Him, the freer you'll find you are to reaching your true potential.

Don't be fooled. Put your hand in God's hand and let Him show you just how good things look from the mountaintop.

Trust in God and you are never to be confounded
in time or in eternity.

DWIGHT LYMAN MOODY

YOUR DAILY REFLECTIONS

_____

_____

_____

_____

*If you need wisdom—if you want to know what God wants
you to do—ask him, and he will gladly tell you.*

JAMES 1:5 NLT

When you're faced with a tough decision, it's only
natural to go to a friend for advice. Chatting
openly with someone who knows you and your situation
well can help you put the pros and cons of your options into
a clearer perspective. So, what could make more sense than
spending time talking things over with God—the One who
knows you better than anyone else?

God cares about the direction your life is headed. The
decisions you make each day help determine that direction.
Weighing your decisions by what's written in the Bible and
with the wisdom God provides for the asking will not only
help you determine right from wrong, but better from
best.

Simply wait upon him. So doing, we shall be directed,
supplied, protected, corrected, and rewarded.

VANCE HAVNER

YOUR DAILY REFLECTIONS

_____

_____

_____

_____

See that you go on growing in the Lord, and become strong and vigorous in the truth you were taught.

COLOSSIANS 2:7 TLB

Being "grown" doesn't mean you stop growing. Every single day of your life, from the moment you were conceived until the day you meet Jesus face-to-face, you have been growing into the person God created you to be.

Just like any thriving plant, how well you grow is partially dependent on the quality of the soil you're planted in. When you're firmly rooted in God—in what He says is right and good and true, in your relationship with Him, and in your relationships with others—you will have rich, fertile soil in which to hold on tight and reach for the sky. Then make sure you get plenty of water each day by praying and reading God's Word—the Bible.

Progress in the Christian life is exactly equal
to the growing knowledge we gain of
the Triune God in personal experience.

A. W. TOZER

YOUR DAILY REFLECTIONS

_____

_____

_____

_____

The LORD hates cheating, but he delights in honesty.
PROVERBS 11:1 NLT

You don't have to be on the FBI's Most Wanted List to be dishonest. All you have to do is exaggerate a personal story to make yourself look better in your friends' eyes. Eat a few grapes before you pay for the bunch at the grocery store. Record your weight a few pounds lower than reality on a health insurance form.

Dishonesty is a habit that's easy to fall into. But, honesty is a gift you can give to the God who loves you. It's also a way to simplify your life. Being honest means never having to keep track of lies you've told or look over your shoulder, wondering if you'll get caught. It means people and God can trust you and your word. And that's the truth!

As honesty and real integrity characterize our lives, there will be no need to manipulate others.
CHARLES R. SWINDOLL

YOUR DAILY REFLECTIONS

_____

_____

_____

_____

Your constant love reaches above the heavens;
your faithfulness touches the skies.

PSALM 108:4 GNT

"I love you" is a phrase everyone longs to hear. However, real love is evident without a word having to be said. It's seen in the attention, affection, and sacrifice people show for the ones they care about.

If you want to know how much God loves you, just look at what He's done. When Jesus died on the cross, He was saying, "I love you," more beautifully than it's ever been said before. But, God's love didn't stop there. He listens to your prayers as if you were the only person in the world. He brings good things into your life, even out of seemingly impossible situations. God's love for you will not end. It'll only grow deeper as you grow closer to Him.

God does not love us because we are valuable.
We are valuable because God loves us.

FULTON JOHN SHEEN

YOUR DAILY REFLECTIONS

_____

_____

_____

_____

Be still before the LORD and wait patiently for him.

PSALM 37:7 NIV

Waiting at a red light can drive you nuts. It seems like wasted time—especially if you happen to be in a hurry. But, life is filled with metaphorical red lights. God puts some of them right in front of you on purpose—to slow you down, so you'll wait on Him.

Waiting for God's "green light" in any situation teaches you patience. It reminds you that some things are simply out of your control. It prompts you to stay close in prayer. It protects you by giving you time to mature. It opens your eyes to things you might have missed in your hurry to move further and faster down the road of life. As you're waiting patiently, God is working purposefully.

He who possesses patience, possesses himself.

RAYMOND LULL

YOUR DAILY REFLECTIONS

_____

_____

_____

_____

Wisdom is a tree of life to those who embrace her;
happy are those who hold her tightly.

PROVERBS 3:18 NLT

You don't have to be old to be wise. A lot of old people do really stupid things. But then again, so do a lot of young people. Being wise has less to do with age and IQ than with your ability to apply what God has taught you to your everyday life. Application takes thought, prayer, and effort.

But to apply something, first you have to know it. As you read the Bible, ask God to help you understand what His words meant to the people they were originally written for, then what they mean for you individually. (A "life application" or study Bible can help.) Then, put what God teaches you into practice. The more you do, the wiser you and your actions will become.

Knowledge comes, but wisdom lingers.

ALFRED LORD TENNYSON

YOUR DAILY REFLECTIONS

_____

_____

_____

_____

Shine out among them like beacon lights,
holding out to them the Word of Life.

PHILIPPIANS 2:15–16 TLB

Regardless of how you spend your time—whether you are a professional person, a stay-at-home mom, or a retiree—you have many opportunities each day to affect the lives of other people. It's a wonderful opportunity and responsibility.

Ask God each day to make you more aware of those around you and their needs—the checker at the grocery store, the elderly gentleman at the bus stop, or the repairman who comes to fix your dryer. Everyone needs to feel God's love, and someone is waiting to feel His touch through you. Don't disappoint. God is counting on you to be His hands and feet—His tender voice, His heart of compassion.

The way from God to a human heart
is through a human heart.

SAMUEL GORDON

YOUR DAILY REFLECTIONS

_____

_____

_____

_____

With God's power working in us, God can do much,
much more than anything we can ask or imagine.

EPHESIANS 3:20 NCV

You've been waiting for months for the release of the sequel to your favorite movie. Finally, the time has come. You've waited in line, purchased your ticket, and found yourself a seat. You have an idea of what lies ahead, but you don't exactly know what's going to happen. All you know is that it's bound to be great.

That's the kind of expectation you can have about the life God has planned for you. He is more creative than any filmmaker, more amazing than any special effect, and more loving than any cinematic hero. You may not fully understand your story's beauty until you've reached the finale, but God promises every detail of the plot has been chosen for your ultimate good.

There is something new every day if you look for it.

HANNAH HURNARD

YOUR DAILY REFLECTIONS

_____

_____

_____

_____

As iron sharpens iron, a friend sharpens a friend.
PROVERBS 27:17 NLT

Life is filled with change—job changes, moves across country, pursuing the purposes God has for you. That might mean seeing less of someone who has come to be a friend. But it doesn't have to mean saying good-bye.

Keeping in touch when you no longer work or live nearby takes effort, but it can be done. An e-mail, crazy card, or heartfelt phone call is all you need to keep your friendship alive and spark many happy reunions. The friends God brings into your life are worth holding on to—and praying for. When it comes to friendship, "out of sight" does not have to mean "out of mind." No matter where change takes you, you can keep your friends close to your heart.

Many a friendship—long, loyal, and self-sacrificing—
rested at first upon no thicker a foundation
than a kind word.
FREDERICK W. FABER

YOUR DAILY REFLECTIONS

_____

_____

_____

_____

Obscene stories, foolish talk, and coarse jokes—
these are not for you.

EPHESIANS 5:4 NLT

Picture Jesus as your constant companion, accompanying you for coffee with your friends, watching a DVD together late into the night, cheering alongside you in the bleachers at a sporting event, or dropping by a convenience store to pick up a magazine. Does knowing that Jesus is right beside you influence the choices you make or the language you use?

If there is any part of your life you'd be embarrassed for Jesus to see or hear, your purity may be in jeopardy. It's easy to forget that God grieves when you go along with the crowd—or your own less-than-pure desires—and do something you know you shouldn't. Dare to do what's right. Choose to keep your heart and life pure.

Only a passionate love of purity
can save a man from impurity.

WILLIAM BARCLAY

YOUR DAILY REFLECTIONS

_____

_____

_____

_____

God will deliver the needy who cry out,
the afflicted who have no one to help.

PSALM 72:12 NIV

A simple, one-word prayer is often the most heartfelt. But, brevity doesn't bother God. He knows exactly what you need—and it may differ considerably from what you want. You may want circumstances to change immediately or even for time to reverse itself.

Though God can and does work miracles, usually His help comes in subtler ways, such as a renewal of strength, an outpouring of hope, or a peace that passes understanding. It may come through the words of a friend, the kindness of a stranger, or the awesome wonder of a thunderstorm. The help God offers varies from situation to situation. But, one thing that never varies is God's dependability in answering your heartfelt prayers.

Jesus promised his followers that "The Strengthener"
would be with them. This promise is no lullaby
for the fainthearted. It is a blood transfusion
for courageous living.

E. PAUL HOVEY

YOUR DAILY REFLECTIONS

_____

_____

_____

Jesus said, "Real life is not measured by how much we own."
LUKE 12:15 NLT

With every step you take in life, budgets, taxes, and bottom lines become more and more important. The challenge is to prevent what you own from owning you.

A rich life is not measured in paychecks or possessions. It's measured by the depth of your relationships with God and others. Handling money wisely by spending within your budget, using credit cautiously, saving for the future, and giving generously as God's Word directs, will help you keep money in perspective. It's just a tool, not a true treasure. Ask God to help you manage what you have, no matter how much or little that is, in a way that honors Him.

Money can buy the husk of many things
but not the kernel.

HENRIK IBSEN

YOUR DAILY REFLECTIONS

_____

_____

_____

_____

Because of the LORD's great love we are not consumed,
for his compassions never fail. They are new every morning.
LAMENTATIONS 3:22–23 NIV

Has there ever been a time in your life when you offended someone—said or did something wrong—and though you asked, that person would not accept your apology? The relationship never got a second chance. That happens sometimes with people, but never with God.

When you blow it, make a poor choice, or even all-out rebel, God says, "Let's begin again." He is always ready to forgive. All He asks is that you come to Him in honest repentance and ask for His forgiveness. From that moment, the past truly is history. All is forgiven.

God is all about second chances and fresh, new beginnings.

Each day is a new life. Seize it. Live it.
DAVID GUY POWERS

YOUR DAILY REFLECTIONS

_____

_____

_____

_____

Every good and perfect gift is from above,
coming down from the Father of the heavenly lights,
who does not change like shifting shadows.

JAMES 1:17 NIV

When you think about counting your blessings, your mind most likely turns to those you can see—a warm place to live, food in the fridge, friends and family to hold you close. But, the blessings God showers on you every day go far beyond what you can touch with your hands.

God's blessings include miracles like the process of prayer, a future home in Heaven, and God's ultimate gift of salvation. Although blessings like these are really more than the human mind can understand, they are also easily taken for granted. Take time right now to send God a heartfelt thank-you note, via prayer. Ask Him to help your gratitude grow by making you increasingly aware of every blessing He brings your way.

The more we count the blessings we have,
the less we crave the luxuries we haven't.

WILLIAM ARTHUR WARD

YOUR DAILY REFLECTIONS

_____

_____

_____

_____

Let your constant love comfort me, as you have promised me.
PSALM 119:76 GNT

Everyone weeps. Even if your tears are not visible to those around you, life on this imperfect earth is bound to break your heart now and then. But, you have a Father who loves you deeply. He doesn't want your heart to remain in shattered pieces. Like a mother who runs to her child's side the moment she hears a pain-filled cry, God is near, offering tender comfort when you need it most.

When you're in distress, cry out to God. He'll never put you down for being overly emotional or tell you to grow up. Instead, He'll go to the source of your heartbreak, soothing your soul with peace and perspective. Allow God to dry your tears with His love.

In Christ the heart of the Father is revealed,
the higher comfort there cannot be
than to rest in the Father's heart.
ANDREW MURRAY

YOUR DAILY REFLECTIONS

_____

_____

_____

_____

*Cheerfully share your home with those who need
a meal or a place to stay.*

1 PETER 4:9 NLT

You don't have to own a house to make someone feel at home. All you have to do is open your heart. That's what hospitality is all about. It has nothing to do with your gourmet cooking skills or opulent guest accommodations. Cheerfully sharing what you have—be it little or much—is the only rule.

So, relax. Welcome in friends both old and new. Ask lots of questions and listen thoughtfully to their answers. Don't try to impress visitors with your possessions or culinary expertise. Warm them with genuine care and affection. The more you see guests, even unexpected ones, as a blessing rather than an inconvenience, the more you'll enjoy the adventure of opening your home and heart to others.

Who practices hospitality entertains God himself.

AUTHOR UNKNOWN

YOUR DAILY REFLECTIONS

_____

_____

_____

_____

In everything you do, put God first,
and he will direct you and crown
your efforts with success.

PROVERBS 3:6 TLB

Personal success cannot be measured by the make of your car, the size of your paycheck, or even the recognition you receive for a job well done. True success depends on who you are, not on what you've accomplished.

God created you with a unique potential that only you can fulfill. The more you focus on becoming who God intended you to be, the more successful you'll become—no matter what career path you choose.

Use the gifts God's given you to the best of your ability, and ask God to guide you in making wise choices. Seek God's approval more than the approval of those around you. Then, your success will be certain.

Success is a journey, not a destination.

BEN SWEETLAND

YOUR DAILY REFLECTIONS

_____

_____

_____

_____

Live a life worthy of the calling you have received.
Be completely humble and gentle.

EPHESIANS 4:1–2 NIV

Remember wrestling on the floor when you were a kid? The inevitable parental warning usually went something like this: "Don't play rough or someone's going to get hurt!" That same warning holds true today. Anytime you interact with another person, there's a chance that someone may get hurt. That's why being gentle with one another is so important.

It doesn't matter if you're a big, burly guy or a gal who's never met a risk she didn't want to take. Gentleness is not a personality trait. It's a character quality worth putting into practice.

Whoever you spend time with today—friends, family, and strangers alike—play gently. Let your words, your tone of voice, your actions, and even your attitude reflect a tender, godly spirit.

Feelings are everywhere ... be gentle.

J. MASAI

YOUR DAILY REFLECTIONS

_____

_____

_____

_____

Since you are so eager to have spiritual gifts,
ask God for those that will be of real help to the whole church.
1 CORINTHIANS 14:12 NLT

There's a church out there that needs you. It isn't complete without you. What awaits is a support group of friends, an opportunity to use the gifts God's given you, and an environment where you can grow. But, you have to make the first move.

The best way to find a good church is to ask a friend if he or she is happy in the church they attend. If so, then ask if you can go along. If you're already part of a church, check your involvement level. If you're over- or under-involved, ask God to help you find a healthy balance. Honor God and feed your own hungry soul by attending a weekly service. Go with a teachable mind and a servant's heart—and enjoy.

The church is an organism, not an organization;
a movement, not a monument.

CHARLES COLSON

YOUR DAILY REFLECTIONS

_____

_____

_____

_____

God's truth stands firm like a foundation stone
with this inscription:
"The Lord knows those who are his."

2 TIMOTHY 2:19 NLT

There are not many things in life that can be considered totally secure and immovable. However, the ground is usually one of them. Yet, all it takes is a shifting fault line to remind you that even the solid foundation beneath your feet is not fully trustworthy.

God has no fault lines. His promises, power, truth, and love are your only true security. When the world around you starts to shake, relationships shift, your health crumbles, or your finances threaten to fall off the deep end, remind yourself of who you're leaning on for support. Rest the full weight of your troubles on the all-powerful God. He's a foundation that will never fail.

A little from God is better than a great deal from men.
What is from men is uncertain and is often lost
and tumbled over and over by men;
but what is from God is fixed as a nail in a sure place.

JOHN BUNYAN

YOUR DAILY REFLECTIONS

_____

_____

_____

_____

Jesus said, "A good person produces
good words from a good heart."
MATTHEW 12:35 NLT

You don't have to be a genius to know that an apple tree produces apples. You wouldn't expect it to produce watermelons or kumquats. It only produces fruit in keeping with the kind of tree it is.

Your heart is the same way. It produces words that reflect the "kind" of heart you have. Sure, you can fake it for a while. You can try to sound sweet and sincere when your heart is really filled with anger or pride. But, eventually that "natural" fruit is going to blossom.

Watching your words begins with examining your own heart. Ask God if you have any negative attitudes that need to be uprooted. With His help, you can consistently give words of love, instead of carelessly tossing rotten verbal apples.

Good words are worth much, and cost little.
GEORGE HERBERT

YOUR DAILY REFLECTIONS

God looked over all that he had made,
and it was excellent in every way.

GENESIS 1:31 TLB

To better understand the heart of an artist, you need to study his work. Examine his brush strokes. Note his favorite color palette. Consider his subject matter. Not to mention, just sit and enjoy the beauty of his creation.

God is the ultimate artist. His creations are so amazing that a lifetime is not long enough to fully appreciate them. However, you can understand God's heart a little better by studying His work. Even the simplest butterfly shows His creativity, attention to detail, organizational skills, and love of beauty.

Wherever you are right now, take a quick peek outside. What does what you see teach you about the God you cannot see? Take a moment to tell God what you think about His handiwork.

Jesus taught men to see the operation of God
in the regular and the normal—in the rising of the sun
and the falling of the rain and the growth of the plant.

WILLIAM TEMPLE

YOUR DAILY REFLECTIONS

_____

_____

_____

_____

I will rejoice in the LORD, I will be joyful in God my Savior.
HABAKKUK 3:18 NIV

When a baby sees his mother's face, every part of his body wiggles, jiggles, and smiles with delight. His source of joy is the one he loves, the one he recognizes—even at an early age—the one who loves him in return.

Growing in your relationship with God is not just an exercise in getting to know the Bible better. It is all about getting to know God better, up close and personal. He wants to be the source of your joy and delight.

Even when circumstances are anything but happy, true joy is as close as God's loving presence. Spend time talking to Him, finding comfort in His promises and contentment in His love. There is no deeper joy this side of Heaven.

Joy is the most infallible sign of the presence of God.
LÉON BLOY

YOUR DAILY REFLECTIONS

_____

_____

_____

_____

I am the LORD, who heals you.

EXODUS 15:26 NIV

Your body is an incredible gift, but it's not an indestructible one. Bodies break down, wear out, and catch all kinds of diseases. Even if you take good care of yourself—eat a balanced diet, get enough sleep, exercise regularly—God doesn't guarantee your body will always run smoothly.

When your health goes downhill, get God involved. He doesn't discourage you from seeking medical treatment. He simply encourages you to turn to Him as part of the healing process, recognizing that He is the source of all true healing. And when God heals, He goes deeper than your physical body. He can also bring healing to your spirit and soul as well. God knows all about you. Trust Him to heal you in the way He knows is best.

The all-sufficient Physician of humanity, the Savior, heals both our body and soul, which are the proper man.

CLEMENT OF ALEXANDRIA

YOUR DAILY REFLECTIONS

_____

_____

_____

_____

Guard my words as your most precious possession.
PROVERBS 7:2 TLB

The Bible isn't homework. It's not a textbook you have to study or an assignment you need to complete. It's a love letter from Someone who cherishes His eternal relationship with you.

So, read the Bible like you do a letter from a close friend. Don't hurry through it. Savor it. See if your Friend has any requests you need to fulfill or advice for you to follow. See if what's said reveals anything new about how your Friend views you, others, or world situations. Then, respond with a love note of your own, written in the words of a heartfelt prayer.

This great book, the Bible, this most precious volume
is the heart of God made legible;
it is the gold of God's love,
beaten out into gold leaf.

JOHN BUNYAN

YOUR DAILY REFLECTIONS

_____

_____

_____

_____

Whenever you stand praying, if you have anything against anyone, forgive him, that your Father in heaven may also forgive you your trespasses.

MARK 11:25

A grudge is a heavy weight to carry. It can affect your thoughts, your attitude, and even your health. You can't get rid of it by simply trying to forget you've been hurt. You have to replace it with something that heals the pain. That "something" is forgiveness.

Forgiving someone doesn't excuse what happened or automatically mend a relationship. It doesn't mean you're "weak" for giving in. It means you're strong enough to imitate God's character, courageous enough to practice real love toward someone who may not deserve it. That's something that requires God's help.

If there's a grudge currently weighing on you, go to God. Ask Him to help you honestly forgive—and let the healing begin.

When you forgive, you in no way change the past—
but you sure do change the future.

BERNARD MELTZER

YOUR DAILY REFLECTIONS

_____

_____

_____

_____

Behave courageously, and the Lord will be with the good.
2 CHRONICLES 19:11

Courage is probably not something you think of as being displayed in everyday life. It is a word that seems to be reserved mostly for war heroes or characters in a movie. But courage is more common than you might think.

The dictionary defines "courage" as the ability to face something dangerous, difficult, or painful and deal with it. You have probably done that many times without realizing you were being brave. Perhaps you have sat by the bed of a dying friend, faced a negative pattern in your life, or forgiven an erring spouse. All those things required courage.

God knows that it would be easier to run and hide than to deal courageously with some of the situations life sends your way. He's proud of you.

Courage is the first of human qualities because
it is the quality that guarantees all others.
WINSTON CHURCHILL

YOUR DAILY REFLECTIONS

_____

_____

_____

_____

Let us run the race before us and never give up.
HEBREWS 12:1 NCV

In track and field, there are a few common-sense tips to winning a race: Stay in shape. Stay alert. Pace yourself. Keep your eyes on the goal. Never give up.

Life can feel like a very long race at times. It's easy to get tired or discouraged when obstacles get in your way or when it feels as though the people running next to you would rather see you fail than succeed. But, God has a race that's set just for you. It's not a saunter through the park. It's a race that will push you to your full potential. But, keep moving. God is cheering you on, every step of the way.

By perseverance the snail reached the ark.
CHARLES HADDON SPURGEON

YOUR DAILY REFLECTIONS

_____

_____

_____

_____

Ask where the good way is, and walk in it.

JEREMIAH 6:16 NIV

"Good" seems like a relative term. Ice cream is good. So are the Broncos. You can have a good attitude, good penmanship, or get a good deal on a used car. Some people even preach, "If it feels good, do it!"

The best way to know what is truly good is to remove an "o" from the word "good" itself. All that remains is God. Whatever God would do, say, or praise in any given situation is what is wholly good.

Being a genuinely good person means being a godly person. That is someone whose heart and actions make God smile. Make that your measure of having a "good" day.

Think of how good God is! He gives us the physical, mental, and spiritual ability to work in his kingdom, and then he rewards us for doing it!

ERWIN W. LUTZER

YOUR DAILY REFLECTIONS

_____

_____

_____

_____

Before they call, I will answer;
and while they are yet speaking, I will hear.

ISAIAH 65:24 KJV

You don't need words to talk to God. Tears, sighs, and even silence can communicate with your heavenly Father in the same way that a look on your face can communicate what you're feeling to a friend. Those who know you well can understand what runs even deeper than words, just by being in your presence.

The Creator of the universe is always in your presence—although that's easy to forget at times. Even though He knows your every thought, prayer reminds you that God is near. It prompts you to include Him in every detail of your day, even the little ones.

When you wake up, before you fall asleep, whether you're feeling fearful or joyful—anytime is the right time to talk to God.

When you can't put your prayers into words,
God hears your heart.

AUTHOR UNKNOWN

YOUR DAILY REFLECTIONS

_____

_____

_____

_____

*A faithful employee is as refreshing
as a cool day in the hot summertime.*

PROVERBS 25:13 TLB

When you look back at the years of work you have behind you, you can feel proud of everything you've achieved. But, there's so much more for you to accomplish. Don't let the thought of all the work that's ahead discourage you. Let it inspire you.

Work is more than something you do to pay the bills. It's a way of making a positive impact on the world around you and reflecting God's example of excellence. It's also an opportunity to use the unique combination of gifts and talents God has given you.

It doesn't matter whether you work on Wall Street or at a drive-through window. Put your whole heart into whatever you do. God can use your efforts to do great things.

There's no labor a man can do that's undignified,
if he does it right.

BILL COSBY

YOUR DAILY REFLECTIONS

_____

_____

_____

_____

How rich is God's grace,
which he has given to us so fully and freely.

EPHESIANS 1:7–8 NCV

Grace is the ultimate free gift. You don't deserve it. You can't earn it. It will never wear out or grow thin. It fits you perfectly, no matter who you are. All you have to do to receive this life-changing gift is ask for it.

Even though this gift is free, that doesn't mean it didn't come at a high price. But, God and His Son felt you were worth it. Jesus gave His life so that God's grace could change yours—not only your life here on Earth, but throughout eternity.

Take a moment to think about God's gift of grace—and what it cost to extend it so freely to you. Thank God for the difference it's made in your life.

Grace is always given to those ready to give thanks for it.

THOMAS À KEMPIS

YOUR DAILY REFLECTIONS

_____

_____

_____

_____

Think of ways to encourage one another
to outbursts of love and good deeds.

HEBREWS 10:24 NLT

Encouragement is more than building others up with your words. It's helping them find the courage to move ahead in a positive direction.

When God opens your eyes to someone who's discouraged, disappointed, or in need of comfort, ask Him for the wisdom to know the best words and actions to share. Then, let God's love for you encourage your own heart so that you can reach out in confidence, kindness, and humility.

Whatever you do or say, remember that it's God's love and power working through you that ultimately helps another person—not your own superior counseling abilities. When God uses you in the lives of others, always thank Him for the privilege of being an encourager.

Encouragement costs you nothing to give,
but it is priceless to receive.

AUTHOR UNKNOWN

YOUR DAILY REFLECTIONS

_____

_____

_____

_____

If you honor your father and mother,
"you will live a long life, full of blessing."

EPHESIANS 6:3 NLT

You may have been living away from home for years or just a short time. Either way, you know that when your address changes, your relationship with your parents also goes through a transition. As always, God provides guidelines for handling the relational challenges of being an adult child.

No matter what your age, God asks that you honor your parents. Period. He doesn't add "if they deserve it" or "until you leave home." Honor is to be a lifelong gift from you to your parents. And as you may already know, it's a gift you may need God's help to give. Call on Him. He will help you discover those qualities you can applaud in your mother and father and show you creative ways to honor them.

As the family goes, so goes the nation
and so goes the whole world in which we live.

POPE JOHN PAUL II

YOUR DAILY REFLECTIONS

_____

_____

_____

_____

You have been my hope, O Sovereign LORD,
my confidence since my youth.

PSALM 71:5 NIV

The first rule of any job interview is "act confident." Does that confidence come from your education? Your natural abilities? Your family connections? The new designer suit you're wearing?

Confidence in anything other than God's love for you and His power working through you is not sturdy enough to build an accurate self-image on. Self-assurance is great, but God-assurance will keep you going through the ups and downs of life.

When you're faced with a challenge, thank God for the strengths and assets He's provided you with. Then, refuse to rely solely on them. Firmly place your confidence in God—who He is and who He says you are in Him.

Our confidence in Christ does not make us lazy,
negligent, or careless, but, on the contrary,
it awakens us, urges us on, and makes us active
in living righteous lives and doing good.

ULRICH ZWINGLI

YOUR DAILY REFLECTIONS

_____

_____

_____

_____

Those who are generous are blessed,
for they share their bread with the poor.

PROVERBS 22:9 NRSV

Picture a miser. Someone like Ebenezer Scrooge will do. He holds on tightly to everything he owns. He's focused on his own needs, the value of his possessions, what he hopes to attain—never on the needs of others. The struggles of those around him do nothing to move his heart. That's because his heart is totally wrapped up in himself.

Now, picture a person whose life is exactly the opposite. That's generosity in action. Holding on to money and possessions loosely. Recognizing that everything you have is a gift, making it easy to share those gifts with others. Being other-centered, instead of self-centered.

While being miserly leads to misery, generosity leads to true wealth—the joy of a life rich in relationship, community, and contentment.

A generous action is its own reward.

WILLIAM WALSH

YOUR DAILY REFLECTIONS

I pondered the direction of my life,
and I turned to follow your statutes.

PSALM 119:58 NLT

What do you do when your heart is tugging you one way, but you know God is telling you to go in exactly the opposite direction? Trust God. The guidelines He has given you in the Bible do not change, no matter what the circumstances. What He says is always true, always right, always wise.

Your heart, however well intentioned, can be swayed by emotion, public opinion, even things like exhaustion or pride. It's not a trustworthy compass when it comes to leading you in the right direction.

When a decision comes down to following your heart or following God, you don't need to ask for directions. There's only one right way to go.

You can never go wrong when you choose to obey Christ.

AUTHOR UNKNOWN

YOUR DAILY REFLECTIONS

_____

_____

_____

_____

Honor God by accepting each other,
as Christ has accepted you.

ROMANS 15:7 CEV

God accepts you—warts and all. Can you do the same for those around you? It's easy to get distracted. A different race, different religious beliefs, even a different style of clothes can lead you to make judgments before you even carry on a conversation with someone.

The key is to bypass what you see and focus on what you know. God created each person with great love and care. God accepts each person, even if he or she has not accepted Him. The more you learn to view others through God's love—instead of sizing them up with your eyes—the easier it will be to accept them as equals, treat them as friends, and love them as God's precious children.

Just as I am, thou wilt receive, will welcome,
pardon, cleanse, relieve; because thy promise I believe,
O Lamb of God, I come.

CHARLOTTE ELLIOTT

YOUR DAILY REFLECTIONS

_____

_____

_____

_____

Fear not, for I am with you; be not dismayed,
for I am your God. I will strengthen you, yes, I will help you,
I will uphold you with My righteous right hand.

ISAIAH 41:10

It takes courage to go where God leads. He'll often take you right to the doorstep of your greatest fears, put you face-to-face with someone you can't stand to be around, or bring a situation into your life that seems impossible to work out. Don't panic. Those are the times when you can really see God's power in action.

You were never created to handle tough times alone. Consider David. The only reason he could conquer a giant was because God was with Him. You have the same advantage. God is fighting every battle with you, never against you.

So, take courage. Stand up to the giants in your life. With God's help, victory is at hand.

Courage faces fear and thereby masters it.

MARTIN LUTHER KING JR.

YOUR DAILY REFLECTIONS

_____

_____

_____

_____

The wisdom of the prudent is to give thought to their ways.

PROVERBS 14:8 NIV

Every action, attitude, and plan for the future begins in one place—your mind. That's why God cares so much about what's going on in your cranium. What you spend time thinking about determines what you will spend time doing—and ultimately who you will become.

Before you knew God, your thoughts pretty much centered around one thing—You. Meeting your own needs. Keeping yourself happy. But, times have changed. And your thoughts should have changed too.

Notice where you let your mind wander. If it heads down any road you feel God would prefer that you not go, consciously change directions. If certain activities negatively influence your thoughts, find alternative ways to spend your time. Changing your mind really can change your life.

Keep your thoughts right, for as you think, so are you.

HENRY H. BUCKLEY

YOUR DAILY REFLECTIONS

_____

_____

_____

_____

Do not think of yourself more highly than you ought,
but rather think of yourself with sober judgment,
in accordance with the measure of faith God has given you.

ROMANS 12:3 NIV

Unlike what you see in the movies, humility is a good thing. It isn't putting yourself down or trying to blend in with the wallpaper. Humility is simply seeing yourself from God's point of view. It's accepting that you're worth no more—or less—than any other person.

Once you have a clear view of yourself, you can get a clearer view of what God wants you to do. You won't argue over what you think is too hard for you to tackle or way beneath your dignity. You can do whatever God asks—and rest in knowing that with God, your best is always good enough.

True humility is not an abject, groveling,
self-despising spirit; it is but a right estimate
of ourselves as God sees us.

TRYON EDWARDS

YOUR DAILY REFLECTIONS

_____

_____

_____

_____

May the Lord make you increase and abound
in love to one another and to all, just as we do to you.

1 THESSALONIANS 3:12

Want to know what love looks like? Look at God. Consider His sacrifice, His patience, His comfort, His faithfulness, His generosity. God's creativity in expressing love is so great that it's almost incomprehensible.

Consider how your love stands up next to His. Don't get discouraged. You're not God. At times, your love still falters and fails. But, God's love is at work in your life. He's helping you love others in the same wonderful way He so deeply loves you.

Let God's creative compassion inspire you to love others well. Ask His help in knowing the best way to express your love so that it meets needs, builds relationships, and warms hearts. Then, take a moment to sit back and enjoy His love for you.

Love is the thing that makes life possible
or, indeed, tolerable.

ARNOLD JOSEPH TOYNBEE

YOUR DAILY REFLECTIONS

_____

_____

_____

_____

I will refresh the weary and satisfy the faint.
JEREMIAH 31:24 NIV

Imagine carrying a heavy backpack around with you everywhere you go. Now imagine that people are always asking you to carry their backpacks as well. Impossible? You bet. Your back was not designed to carry that kind of load.

When life starts weighing on you like an overstuffed backpack, chances are that you may be carrying more than God intended for you. Take the load to God. Lay it out before Him. Ask Him what to pick back up and what to leave behind. Lean on Him for strength with any especially heavy problems.

Then, rest against God's strong arms. Close your eyes for just a few minutes and enjoy a mini-retreat. God's presence can lighten the heaviest heart.

Unless we come apart and rest a while,
we may just plain come apart.
VANCE HAVNER

YOUR DAILY REFLECTIONS

_____

_____

_____

_____

Let me be weighed on honest scales,
that God may know my integrity.

JOB 31:6

When storms begin to blow, the integrity of a building is revealed—the strength of its foundation, the practicality of its design, and the quality of its building materials. Will it stand or will it fall?

The same holds true for your own integrity. When the pressure is on, weak spots in your faith or character readily come to light. If this happens, take note. Your integrity matures over time. If you've made choices that weren't sound in the past, make better choices today. Make sure your foundation rests solely on what God says is true, not on what your emotions or contemporary culture says is right.

Then, turn your face toward the wind with confidence. You and your integrity are built to last.

Integrity has no need of rules.

ALBERT CAMUS

YOUR DAILY REFLECTIONS

_____

_____

_____

_____

These are evil times, so make every minute count.

EPHESIANS 5:16 CEV

You only get one "today." After 1,440 minutes, your today becomes a yesterday. No do-overs, no second chances, no turning back the clock. Choosing how you'll spend the time you have is a big responsibility. You can waste it on what is worthless or invest it in what will last throughout eternity. The choice is yours.

God wants you to live life to the fullest. That begins with making wise, premeditated choices about how you'll spend the days ahead. That doesn't mean you need to book every minute on your calendar or that lying on the beach soaking up a little sun is a waste of time. Just be aware of how easily time slips away—and spend it wisely in light of your priorities.

Time is given us to use in view of eternity.

AUTHOR UNKNOWN

YOUR DAILY REFLECTIONS

_____

_____

_____

_____

God is not a man, that He should lie, nor a son of man,
that He should repent. Has He said, and will He not do?
Or has He spoken, and will He not make it good?

NUMBERS 23:19

As a kid, you probably believed some unbelievable things, like the tooth fairy exchanged molars for cash or Santa shimmied down your chimney on Christmas Eve. Some aspects of God seem unbelievable. But, He's no fairy tale. Put the historicity of Jesus and the faithfulness of God's promises to the test. Know what you believe and why.

Then, don't just say you believe in God, act on that belief. Release guilt and regret, believing God's forgiven you. Risk being authentically you, believing God created you for a unique purpose. Reach out to others, believing love is God's highest aim for your life.

If easy belief is impossible, it is that we may learn
what belief is and in whom it is to be placed.

F. D. MAURICE

YOUR DAILY REFLECTIONS

_____

_____

_____

_____

God satisfies your desires with good things.

PSALM 103:5 NIV

Think about how you feel after a good meal. All your favorite foods filled your plate, and you wisely chose to stop eating before you went from full to stuffed. Then, you sat back and just enjoyed feeling satisfied.

That's how God wants you to feel about life. A job well done, a dream fulfilled, a relationship healed, a confidence in knowing how much God loves you. There are numerous things God can bring your way that will satisfy your heart.

God knows every one of your deepest desires. Trying to fill these desires on your own can lead to frustration—or even lead you away from God. Letting God fill your desires in His way and His time leads to satisfaction that lasts.

There are no days when God's fountain does not flow.

RICHARD OWEN ROBERTS

YOUR DAILY REFLECTIONS

_____

_____

_____

_____

A faithful God who does no wrong, upright and just is he.
DEUTERONOMY 32:4 NIV

"Never" is a tricky word to use properly. It means no exceptions, no chance, no way—ever. But with God, "never" is both accurate and encouraging. God never changes. His promises never fail. His patience never falters. His power never diminishes. His love never ends.

All of these things that will never happen with God are the result of His faithfulness. God is as good as His Word. That means you can count on God, even if others have let you down.

Give God the chance to demonstrate His faithfulness to you. Be bold in following through on what you believe He wants you to do. Then, thank Him for the variety of ways He comes through for you.

Consider seriously how quickly people change,
and how little trust is to be had in them;
and cleave fast unto God, who changeth not.
SAINT TERESA OF AVILA

YOUR DAILY REFLECTIONS

_____

_____

_____

_____

Always try to be kind to each other.

1 THESSALONIANS 5:15 NLT

Kindness is not always soft, quiet, and cuddly. Sometimes it boldly speaks the words someone needs to hear. It stands up for what's right, even when it isn't popular. Kindness does whatever it takes to do what's in the best interest of another.

What gives kindness its gentle strength is love. Every word and action, whether meeting the physical needs of a stranger or confronting a friend on her tendency toward gossip, is motivated by other-centered compassion. Kindness is sensitive to different personality types, creatively crafting an appropriate response for each unique situation. It always leaves pride and judgment behind and reaches out with open, accepting arms to tenderly help another move closer to God. How can you put kindness into action today?

The greatest thing a man can do for his Heavenly Father is to be kind to some of His other children.

HENRY DRUMMOND

YOUR DAILY REFLECTIONS

_____

_____

_____

_____

You, LORD, give perfect peace to those
who keep their purpose firm and put their trust in you.

ISAIAH 26:3 GNT

As every beauty pageant contestant seems to agree, peace—world peace—is one of the deepest desires of the human heart. But what's less frequently understood is that peace is not determined by location or situation. Perfect peace is only found when you trust God, moment by moment, with every situation you face throughout the day.

War, relational conflict, and inner turmoil are all part of life on this earth. But, that doesn't mean the peace on earth God promised is only reserved for Heaven. It's available right now. Ask God to give you a taste of what true peace is like, as you trust in His goodness and rest in His presence.

If the basis of peace is God, the secret of peace is trust.

J. N. FIGGIS

YOUR DAILY REFLECTIONS

_____

_____

_____

_____

If I ride the morning winds to the farthest oceans,
even there your hand will guide me,
your strength will support me.

PSALM 139:9–10 TLB

Wouldn't it be nice to have a Global Positioning System to guide you through life? You could type in your goals—where you want to go—and a friendly voice would advise you as to the best way to get there.

Your relationship with God is better than any GPS on the market. God knows where you've been, where you are, and which direction is best for you to head in the future. God wants you to have access to that same useful information. By reading the Bible, weighing advice from godly friends, and asking God's Spirit to guide you in prayer, you have access to a system of guidance that will never fail, no matter where you roam.

Who brought me hither will bring me hence;
no other guide I seek.

JOHN MILTON

YOUR DAILY REFLECTIONS

_____

_____

_____

_____

If we are living in the light of God's presence,
just as Christ is, then we have fellowship with one another.

1 JOHN 1:7 NLT

"Fellowship" is an old-fashioned-sounding word, bringing to mind potlucks—complete with fat-laden casseroles and colorful gelatin salads—eaten in church basement "fellowship halls." But, true fellowship is never out of date. It's people living on the cutting edge of community, sharing life together. When Christ is the center of that life, that common bond is more than friendship. It's a love that matures through differences and struggles, as well as through praise and play.

To experience fellowship, you have to involve your life with the lives of other people who believe in Christ. You need to risk being real and work your way through problems, instead of running from them. Only then can you experience the joy that being part of God's family brings.

No person is an island, entire of itself;
every person is a piece of the continent,
a part of the main.

JOHN DONNE

YOUR DAILY REFLECTIONS

_____

_____

_____

_____

Know that the LORD, He is God; it is He who has made us,
and not we ourselves; we are His people
and the sheep of His pasture.

PSALM 100:3

In the sixties, young adults were obsessed with "finding themselves." They experimented with drugs, communal living, "free love," and transcendental meditation. Unfortunately, these are ways of losing yourself, rather than finding yourself.

What was true in the sixties is true today. There's only one way to find your true identity—believe what God has to say about you. God says you're loved, forgiven, unique, and eternally significant. As His child, you're also part of a new family that is destined to make a positive impact on this world and the next.

Take a moment to thank God for the many ways He's helping you "find yourself" in Him.

A vital fringe benefit of being a Christian
is the tremendous sense of identity that grows
out of knowing Jesus Christ.

JAMES C. DOBSON

YOUR DAILY REFLECTIONS

_____

_____

_____

_____

*The LORD your God will lead you
and protect you on every side.*

ISAIAH 52:12 GNT

You can eat your vegetables, wear your seat belt, always hike with a buddy, even be a black belt in the martial arts, but there's only one thing that's guaranteed to offer complete protection anytime, anywhere—putting your life fully in God's hands.

That doesn't mean the laws of physics will no longer apply if you drive too fast or that you can act foolishly with no consequence. What it does mean is that when you do your part, you can entrust your life to the heavenly Father who loves you and to the angels He has commissioned to watch over you. Put your life in His hands. He will keep you safe.

In the morning, prayer is the key that opens to us
the treasures of God's mercies and blessings;
in the evening, it is the key that shuts us up
under his protection and safeguard.

JACQUES ELLUL

YOUR DAILY REFLECTIONS

_____

_____

_____

_____

*Provide people with a glimpse of good living
and of the living God.*

PHILIPPIANS 2:15 THE MESSAGE

You are a walking, talking message of hope. Whether you realize it or not, your character, words, and actions are all preaching a sermon to those you meet along the road of life. The closer you follow God, the more visible He'll be to others through you.

You may never know how wide your influence really goes. An act of kindness, a word of encouragement, or a job well done could be what moves a close friend—or even a stranger—one step closer to knowing God.

Take a moment to thank God for the people who've had a positive influence on your life. Then, ask God to help you become someone else's reason for thanks.

We are the Bibles the world is reading; we are
the creeds the world is needing;
we are the sermons the world is heeding.

BILLY GRAHAM

YOUR DAILY REFLECTIONS

_____

_____

_____

_____

Our soul waits for the LORD;
He is our help and our shield.

PSALM 33:20

Say you're in your backyard learning how to cast your new fishing rod. You encounter a problem, so you call an expert fisherman friend to come over and help. He arrives, takes the rod out of your hands, and says, "I'll take it from here. Go on inside." Walking up your back steps you hear him shout, "And from now on, don't try casting this yourself. I'll do all your casting for you." As the screen door slams behind you, you think, *And all I wanted was some help.*

God is always there to help you, not to elbow you out of your own life. When you think about it, you wouldn't want it any other way.

What other help could we ever need
than that of the Holy Spirit of God?

ANDREA GARNEY

YOUR DAILY REFLECTIONS

_____

_____

_____

_____

The LORD is good and his love endures forever;
his faithfulness continues through all generations.

PSALM 100:5 NIV

God will never waver in His faithfulness toward you. But, faithfulness is not a quality reserved for deity. With God's help, you can be faithful in your relationships with others, as well as with Him.

Just look to Him as your example. Ask yourself, "How would God treat this person?" or "What decision would most likely make God smile?" Whatever your answer, it involves some aspect of mirroring God's faithfulness.

When your promises can be trusted, your commitments can be depended upon, and your friends know they can rely on you to be devoted and true, you're faithfully walking in God's own footsteps.

Nothing is more noble,
nothing more venerable than fidelity.

CICERO

YOUR DAILY REFLECTIONS

_____

_____

_____

_____

*Your life is a journey that you must travel
with a deep consciousness of God.*

1 PETER 1:17 THE MESSAGE

What is the meaning of life? This question has been debated by philosophy classes for centuries. But, guess what? You know the answer. Life is a journey toward, or away from, the heart of God. Keeping that in mind makes even the most ordinary day seem extraordinarily important. And it is.

What you do with today matters. Whether you're riding roller coasters with friends or feeding the hungry at a soup kitchen doesn't matter as much as whether what you're doing is drawing you closer to, or farther away, from the One who loves you most.

Where will life take you? The direction is up to you.

There is no more blessed way of living than
the life of faith upon a covenant-keeping God.

CHARLES HADDON SPURGEON

YOUR DAILY REFLECTIONS

_____

_____

_____

_____

The Lord is my strength and my shield.

PSALM 28:7 NIV

If you want to strengthen your muscles, you work out. You lift weights, increasing your repetitions as time goes by. The same is true for building up your spiritual muscles. As God trusts you with increasingly heavier responsibility and you choose to rely on Him more and more, you'll be able to stand stronger, longer—no matter what the circumstances.

The next time you feel weak or afraid, don't believe what you feel. Listen to what God has to say. Rely on the knowledge that you've been working out with your very own Personal Trainer. God knows just the right exercises to help turn your weaknesses into strengths.

The Lord doesn't promise to give us something
to take so we can handle our weary moments.
He promises us himself. That is all. And that is enough.

CHARLES R. SWINDOLL

YOUR DAILY REFLECTIONS

_____

_____

_____

_____

What does the LORD require of you?
To act justly and to love mercy
and to walk humbly with your God.

MICAH 6:8 NIV

Mercy is the key that sets a prisoner free. It extends grace in place of judgment, forgiveness in place of punishment, honor in place of disdain. It makes no sense, except to a heart filled with God's unconditional love.

Mercy is a gift God asks you to give to others—not because they deserve it, but because of the mercy God has demonstrated in your own life. Ask God to bring to mind anyone who could use a tender touch of His mercy. Depending on how God leads you to bestow this special gift, the one who receives it may never even be fully aware of its extent. But, you will. You'll find that being merciful frees up your own heart to love more authentically.

Mercy imitates God and disappoints Satan.

SAINT JOHN CHRYSOSTOM

YOUR DAILY REFLECTIONS

_____

_____

_____

_____

Commit everything you do to the Lord.

PSALM 37:5 TLB

God is committed to you. He won't bail on His promises or put you on "prayer waiting" because a more important call has come in. He will do what He says.

Before you make a commitment, whether to a relationship, a job, or even to volunteer to serve donuts at church on Sunday mornings, you need to weigh the cost. Ask yourself if your time, energy, resources, and talents are all at a level where you can follow through on your promise. Ask God to help you only make commitments that fit with His purpose and direction for your life.

Then, make one more commitment. Commit whatever you're doing to God. Through success, failure, struggles, and growth, allow Him to help you keep your word.

Unless commitment is made,
there are only promises and hope … but no plans.

PETER DRUCKER

YOUR DAILY REFLECTIONS

_____

_____

_____

_____

Wise people act in keeping with the knowledge they have.

PROVERBS 13:16 NIrV

How much do you know? Do you have a diploma on your wall or some hard-learned life lessons to your credit? If so, make sure that learning continues to work for you.

Putting what you know into practice will help you retain the information you have worked so hard to acquire. If you put what you've learned on the shelf, chances are it will be more or less forgotten as time passes.

The "use it or lose it" principle is true of your knowledge of God as well. If you put God and the Bible on the shelf for a while, you may have to relearn some hard lessons. Who wants to take calculus, or a painful lesson on pride, over again? Put what you know into practice.

Wisdom is knowledge rightly applied.

AUTHOR UNKNOWN

YOUR DAILY REFLECTIONS

_____

_____

_____

_____

You forgive us, so that we should stand in awe of you.
                                              PSALM 130:4 GNT

I magine receiving a gift so overly generous that it leaves you speechless. You've done nothing to earn it. As a matter of fact, at times you've been downright awful to the one who's giving it to you. How does your heart respond?

The forgiveness of God is just such a gift. Your response to that gift, whether you apologize for the past and accept it joyfully with open arms or bury your head in shame and refuse to take what you don't deserve, is your gift to God. Which will it be?

Right now, kneel before the Giver of all good gifts. Meditate on what He's forgiven in your life and what it cost for Him to offer that free gift to you.

When God pardons, he consigns the offense
to everlasting forgetfulness.
                                              MERV ROSELL

YOUR DAILY REFLECTIONS

_____

_____

_____

_____

*Happy is the man who finds wisdom, and the man who
gains understanding; for her proceeds are better than
the profits of silver, and her gain than fine gold.*

PROVERBS 3:12

Your career could be your ticket to a higher income bracket. But, no matter what your future net worth winds up to be, you're rich. You found true wealth the moment you chose to follow God, instead of your own prideful heart.

Whether you choose to enjoy the abundance of those riches or bury that eternal treasure and continue striving for the kind of wealth you can hold in your hands will determine how much you enjoy life—and God.

Consider the priceless riches you possess—love, joy, peace, and hope, to mention just a few. No amount of money can buy treasures like these. Enjoy what you've been given by nurturing a thankful heart. Then, share the wealth by pointing others to God's true treasure.

Better rich in God than rich in gold.

ENGLISH PROVERB

YOUR DAILY REFLECTIONS

_____

_____

_____

_____

It's in Christ that we find out who we are
and what we are living for.

EPHESIANS 1:12 THE MESSAGE

Once upon a time, your goal was to graduate. You set your sights on a date, figured out what was required of you, then set mini-goals for completing every individual assignment along the way. Step-by-step, you made it to where you wanted to be.

To meet a goal of any kind, you need to have a concrete understanding of what it requires. And in order for that met goal to be fulfilling to you, it must be compatible with who God created you to be. God can help you with this. Let Him help you evaluate potential goals that lie ahead and see how they fit into His plan for You. Then, prioritize the steps it will take to reach your goal in a way that honors Him.

Every human being is intended to have a character
of his own; to be what no others are,
and to do what no other can do.

WILLIAM ELLERY CHANNING

YOUR DAILY REFLECTIONS

_____

_____

_____

_____

When people sin, they earn what sin pays—death.
But God gives us a free gift—life forever
in Christ Jesus our Lord.

ROMANS 6:23 NCV

Your life will not end with a death certificate. God has made that null and void. There's true life ahead, at a deeper and more beautiful level than anything you can possibly experience in this world broken by sin.

Life on Earth is really just the beginning—the beginning of eternity. Today is your chance to grow and learn, to get acquainted with God and His creations, to get a small, inviting taste of what's to come.

Take a hold of today with your whole heart. Enjoy it. Explore it. Give yourself fully to living it well. But, never lose sight of eternity. What's ahead will far exceed anything you can see from where you stand right now.

Eternity is not something that begins after you are dead.
It is going on all the time.

CHARLOTTE PERKINS GILMAN

YOUR DAILY REFLECTIONS

_____

_____

_____

_____

I will spend time thinking about your miracles.

PSALM 145:5 NIrV

Meditation gets a bad rap. It gets tied in with the New Age movement, Eastern religion, even weight-loss programs. But, in Old Testament times, God told people to meditate on Him.

Meditating on God—His character, His miracles, and His words as communicated in the Bible—helps you understand more about what God is like. It helps change your thinking and your behavior, from the inside out.

Set aside five uninterrupted minutes today to mediate on God. Choose one quality of His character and think about the difference it makes in your life. Let it lead you to give thanks and praise and draw you closer to the heart of God Himself.

When you meditate, imagine that Jesus Christ in person is about to talk to you about the most important thing in the world. Give him your complete attention.

FRANÇOIS FÉNELON

YOUR DAILY REFLECTIONS

_____

_____

_____

_____

My heart is glad, and my glory rejoices;
my flesh also will rest in hope.

PSALM 16:9

Hope is the perfect life preserver in the midst of any storm. It helps keep your head above water, enabling you to fight off feelings of discouragement and despair. As you catch an occasional glimpse of what lies beyond the waves, it aids in reminding you that help is on the way, even if you can't quite see it all yet. Hope helps you survive.

When storm clouds are gathering on the horizon or a torrential downpour has caught you by surprise, hold fast to hope. Remember how God came through time and time again for people in the Bible. Think about how He's come through for you. Then, meditate on His steadfast promises, your greatest source of hope. Help is on the way.

There is no better or more blessed bondage
than to be a prisoner of hope.

ROY Z. KEMP

YOUR DAILY REFLECTIONS

_____

_____

_____

_____

We ought always to thank God for you, brothers,
and rightly so, because your faith is growing more and more.
2 THESSALONIANS 1:3 NIV

Faith is trust that's put to the test. It acts on what it believes to be true. If you have faith that your best friend can keep a secret, you'll risk being honest about your biggest mistakes and regrets. If you have faith that God really loves you, you'll risk making a decision you believe will honor Him, even if it promises not to be easy.

Faith grows the more you use it, the more you try it on for size. Give God the chance to grow yours. Act on what He's asked you to do. Risk moving out of your comfort zone. Do more than believe with your heart. Move forward in faith, wherever He's leading you.

Faith tells us of things we have never seen
and cannot come to know by our natural senses.
SAINT JOHN OF THE CROSS

YOUR DAILY REFLECTIONS

_____

_____

_____

_____

I have learned to be satisfied with the things
I have and with everything that happens.

PHILIPPIANS 4:1 NCV

How much is enough? To a contented heart, it's as much as God has chosen to provide. To measure your personal level of contentment, complete this sentence: "I would be content if only . . ."

What are the "if onlys" in your life? More money? Being involved in a serious relationship? Losing or gaining weight? Landing the job of your dreams?

There's another name for "if onlys." They're called idols. When your desires move from "it would be nice" to "I can't be happy without," you've chosen to believe something can satisfy you, rather than the only thing that really can—God. Ask Him to reveal any "if onlys" you need to confront. Then, ask Him to show you how to find contentment where you are and with what you have right now.

The utmost we can hope for in this life is contentment.

JOSEPH ADDISON

YOUR DAILY REFLECTIONS

_____

_____

_____

_____

Jesus said, "Your task is to be true, not popular."
LUKE 6:26 THE MESSAGE

Your character is who you are when no one's watching. It's the very best of you and worst of you all rolled into one. One of the goals of maturing is to get your character in line with who God created you to be.

Though there is no one quite like you, there are character qualities you should share with all those who follow God. Traits such as honesty, integrity, generosity, and deep-hearted love should be an essential part of who you are and how you relate in this life as God's child.

But, character develops out of choice, not chance. Choose to work on erasing any traits that don't reflect God's character. Ask God to you to help you develop the qualities most like His own.

Reputation is what men and women think of us.
Character is what God and the angels know of us.
THOMAS PAINE

YOUR DAILY REFLECTIONS

_____

_____

_____

_____

I want you to do whatever will help you serve the Lord best,
with as few distractions as possible.

1 CORINTHIANS 8:35 NLT

How you live your life reflects your true priorities more than any list you may be holding in your head. Suppose your love for others is evident to those who know you—and even those who don't. Suppose you talk to God about both the small things as well as the big ones that you face each and every day. And suppose you make plans for your future based on the big picture of eternity, instead of the small snapshot of daily life. Then, chances are, you're trying to keep God number one in your life.

That isn't something you decide once and then forget. Every morning you need to make a choice—"Who will be number one in my life today—God or me?"

Tell me to what you pay attention,
and I will tell you who you are.

JOSÉ ORTEGA Y GASSET

YOUR DAILY REFLECTIONS

_____

_____

_____

_____

Jesus said, "In my Father's house are many rooms;
if it were not so, I would have told you.
I am going there to prepare a place for you."

JOHN 14:2 NIV

Most likely, you have had at least one graduation day in your life. A graduation is a combination of ceremony, excitement, an ending of one phase, and a brand-new beginning of another. It is a mark of achievement. But, there's a graduation day coming that you may be a little more hesitant to participate in—the day you graduate to eternal life in Heaven after your physical death here on Earth.

It's a little unnerving not knowing what to expect. But, one thing is certain. God has prepared a place just for you—a place where you truly belong.

Anytime the fear of death grabs hold of your heart, just picture meeting God face-to-face, saying good-bye to this life and hello to a whole new level of living.

God's retirement plan is out of this world.

AUTHOR UNKNOWN

YOUR DAILY REFLECTIONS

_____

_____

_____

_____

Continue to reverence the Lord all the time,
for surely you have a wonderful future ahead of you.

PROVERBS 23:18 TLB

You can only grab hold of the future one day at a time. The rest of it's out of your reach. That doesn't mean you can't look forward to it, plan for it, or even daydream about it some. The future is like a preview of coming attractions at the movie theater. You only get a brief glimpse of something that will be coming later.

Today is your main attraction, so use it in a way that draws you closer to God. In that way, you can be sure that your past is forgiven, your present blessed, and your future safely in the hands of Him who knows the beginning from the end.

Enjoy the blessings of this day, if God sends them;
and the evils of it bear patiently and sweetly:
for this day only is ours, we are dead to yesterday,
and we are not yet born to the morrow.

JEREMY TAYLOR

YOUR DAILY REFLECTIONS

_____

_____

_____

_____

He shall see the labor of His soul, and be satisfied.
ISAIAH 53:11

There's nothing quite like putting your all into a project—whether at home or at work—knowing you've done your best, then seeing it turn out right. You get a huge sense of satisfaction from a job well done.

Whether you're building a birdhouse or laboring under the hood of your car, when the job is complete, this feeling of satisfaction wells up inside you. Is that pride? It can be if you start boasting about it. But satisfaction is a God-given emotion: you know that your hard work has paid off, you know that you did the job right.

Savor the moment. Life is full of many frustrations and long-term, loose-ended projects, so enjoy each chunk of satisfaction and accomplishment that comes your way.

Look at a day when you are supremely satisfied at the end.
It's not a day when you lounge around doing nothing.
It's when you've had everything to do, and you've done it.
MARGARET THATCHER

YOUR DAILY REFLECTIONS

*You shaped me first inside, then out; you formed me
in my mother's womb. ...
Body and soul, I am marvelously made!*

PSALM 139:13–14 THE MESSAGE

God loves you and is intimately concerned with your life, to the point that "the very hairs of your head are all numbered" (Matthew 10:30). And He was just as involved right from the beginning with the creation of your spirit, soul, and body.

Who you are is largely determined by your inherited genetic traits and your upbringing, but there is more to you than just that. Body and soul, you are a unique creation of God—known by Him and loved by Him. He designed you the way you are for a reason.

There's always room to improve your character and overcome weaknesses, but it's important to accept and love yourself as the unique person God created you to be.

He who counts the stars and calls them by their names
is in no danger of forgetting His own children.

CHARLES HADDON SPURGEON

YOUR DAILY REFLECTIONS

_____

_____

_____

_____

It is God who gives you power to get wealth.

DEUTERONOMY 8:18

If you're struggling financially, you may wish that you were wealthy, but more money may not be the answer. No matter what your financial status is, a few basic principles should be at work in your life.

First of all, you need to trust God, the ultimate Source of all blessings. Then, consider this: what good is wealth without contentment—the ability to enjoy what you have without always striving for more? And last, but not least, you should be practicing wise financial management.

Above all, remember that life is much more than money and the things money can buy. Wealth is fine if you have it, but most valuable in life are those things that money can't buy.

The real measure of our wealth is how much
we'd be worth if we lost all our money.

JOHN HENRY JOWETT

YOUR DAILY REFLECTIONS

_____

_____

_____

_____

Defend the poor and fatherless;
do justice to the afflicted and needy.

PSALM 82:3

When you see a coworker being harassed or taken advantage of and you speak up about it, you're striving for what's right and just. When a con artist defrauds an elderly lady of her life savings and you call the authorities, it's justice you're seeking.

God is a God of justice. He doesn't turn a blind eye to injustice, and He doesn't want you to. Speaking up or doing something when you see wrong being done is a God-given instinct. Just be sure that it's justice that you seek and not "an-eye-for-an-eye" revenge.

Once you've done what you can, leave matters in the hands of those in authority. And most importantly, always leave them in the hands of God.

If it is thought that justice is with us,
it will give birth to courage.

ELMER DAVIS

YOUR DAILY REFLECTIONS

Every part of Scripture is God-breathed and useful one way
or another—showing us truth ... correcting our mistakes,
training us to live God's way.

2 TIMOTHY 3:16 THE MESSAGE

When you come face-to-face with a dilemma you need to know what's right and wrong, what's acceptable and what is not. You need an authoritative standard by which to measure the issues of life.

The Bible is the ultimate word on what God has determined is truth or error, morally right or wrong. Just as the National Bureau of Standards in Washington, D.C., sets the mark for weights, measurement, time and mass, so you have a spiritual Bureau of Standards and Measurements— the Bible.

Everything that comes into your life must be placed alongside the Scriptures to see how it measures up.

The Bible is God's chart for you to steer by,
to keep you from the bottom of the sea,
and to show you where the harbor is,
and how to reach it without running on rocks and bars.

HENRY WARD BEECHER

YOUR DAILY REFLECTIONS

_____

_____

_____

_____

Whatever things are true, whatever things are noble,
whatever things are just, whatever things are pure ...
meditate on these things.

PHILIPPIANS 4:8

God has given human beings amazing minds, and scientists are still trying to figure out how the process of thinking works. The ability to envision things, dream new concepts, work out problems, and make choices is a gift of God.

Your thoughts are not mere nothings; they are important. Every deed begins with a thought. Even thoughts that don't lead to action color your attitude either positively or negatively and affect your entire outlook—which in turn affects you and others around you.

Dwelling on negative thoughts will drag you down, but the good news is that if you make a habit of choosing to think encouraging, positive, caring thoughts—they will eventually make your whole world better!

Think positively and masterfully, with confidence and faith, and life becomes more secure, more fraught with action, richer in achievement and experience.

EDDIE RICKENBACKER

YOUR DAILY REFLECTIONS

_____

_____

_____

_____

Gracious speech is like clover honey—good taste to the soul,
quick energy for the body.

PROVERBS 16:24 THE MESSAGE

If you were to always blurt out what was on your mind without considering how it would affect others, you'd learn that words have the power to discourage. Your words also have great power to encourage when you take the time to speak kindly, point out a fault gently, or share an inspiring insight.

Encouraging words can breathe life into people who have all but given up. You don't need to be a great motivational speaker; you just need to speak from your heart and ask yourself, "What can I say that would help this person?"

This doesn't mean you need to walk on eggshells around people and not speak the truth. You must speak the truth, but as Ephesians 4:15 says, we are to speak the truth in love.

Speaking without thinking is shooting without aiming.

SIR WILLIAM GURNEY BENHAM

YOUR DAILY REFLECTIONS

_____

_____

_____

_____

Better a patient man than a warrior,
a man who controls his temper than one who takes a city.
PROVERBS 16:32 NIV

You've probably seen some almost exaggerated examples of angry impatience—a fellow worker cursing and throwing tools around or a driver fuming when he or she has to wait an extra thirty seconds in traffic. But all of us need to learn more patience.

Being patient doesn't mean standing around all day. You were designed to be active, to think up solutions, to do your best to make things happen. But some things take time no matter how hard you push, so pace yourself, relax.

Trusting God is a large part of being patient. You have to trust that God will work things out. You have to trust that given time, wisdom, and direction, a solution will be found. So have faith. Have patience.

Patience is bitter, but its fruit is sweet.
JEAN-JACQUES ROUSSEAU

YOUR DAILY REFLECTIONS

_____

_____

_____

_____

As for me, I will walk in my integrity.

PSALM 26:11

It's great when you have friends you can trust with your lawnmower or your secrets. It's wonderful when you have businessmen whom you can trust with your money or children whom you can trust to obey your rules. When you trust people, you trust them for the same reason you trust God—you've learned that they're honest, faithful, and dependable.

Be that kind of person too. Care for your friends' belongings, and they'll continue to lend them to you. Be honest in business, and people will trust you. Keep your promises, and your children will have faith in you.

It's easy to be a person whom others trust. You just have to be trustworthy. It takes consistent effort, but God can help you do it!

Integrity of heart is indispensable.

JOHN CALVIN

YOUR DAILY REFLECTIONS

_____

_____

_____

_____

Jesus said, "These things I command you,
that you love one another."

God's Word contains a number of commandments. But the commands repeated the most often in the New Testament are to love God and to love others.

The Bible says that the overriding rule of life is to love! It is to be the underlying motive for everything you do. Yet it's so easy to get distracted doing even good things. You can get so caught up in observing meaningful traditions, such as purchasing Christmas gifts, that it becomes one more thing on your "To-Do" list, instead of it being done with a loving attitude, stemming from a generous heart.

It's not always easy to make sure that everything you do is motivated by Christ's love, so pray and ask God to help you. He will honor that prayer. Remember, God doesn't expect perfection. But He does expect you to love.

Love is the only spiritual power that can overcome
the self-centeredness that is inherent in being alive.

ARNOLD JOSEPH TOYNBEE

YOUR DAILY REFLECTIONS

_____

_____

_____

_____

*Serve wholeheartedly, as if you were serving the Lord,
not men, because you know that the Lord will
reward everyone for whatever good he does.*

EPHESIANS 6:7–8 NIV

If you love what you do, it's easy to put your heart into it and make sure that you consistently deliver quality work.

But there are times when even work you enjoy becomes just that—plain, hard work. A piece keeps coming back for revisions. Unexpected problems arise. Snags happen. Delays. Pleasure turns into frustration.

Or you may be a person who—because of circumstances you can't control—must work at a job you dislike. Then what motivates you to do your best? Commit your work to God. Do your very best for Him. In that way, you'll be doing a service for yourself as well. You simply cannot lose when you set out to please God.

Work becomes worship when done for the Lord.

AUTHOR UNKNOWN

YOUR DAILY REFLECTIONS

_____

_____

_____

_____

Jesus said, "Invite the poor, the crippled, the lame,
and the blind. Then at the resurrection of the godly,
God will reward you for inviting those who can't repay you."
LUKE 14:13–14 TLB

You can get real pleasure from doing kind things for your spouse, your children, your family, and your friends—helping them when they need help, taking the time to listen, or getting a gift that shows them you care. But, did you know that showing kindness to those outside your circle can bring joy as well?

The Bible says that when you are kind to those who are unable to do anything for you in return, you will be rewarded by God. That's the warm sense of satisfaction you feel when you reach out with kindness to someone who needs your help. It's like God pays you back when the person in question cannot.

So reach out whenever you can and feel the touch of God's hand on your life.

True charity is the desire to be useful to others
without thought of recompense.

EMANUEL SWEDENBORG

YOUR DAILY REFLECTIONS

_____

_____

_____

_____

Pray without ceasing.

1 THESSALONIANS 5:17

If you get up early every morning to spend time praying, that's wonderful! But it could be that finding time in your busy schedule for prayer is a real challenge.

The good news is that you can pray all the time, wherever you are, whatever you're doing. Remember, prayer simply means talking to God, person-to-person, friend-to-friend. He may be the all-powerful Creator of the universe, but He always has time for you. So talk to Him throughout your day. Talk to Him about everything.

You can praise God for His wonders, you can pray for wisdom, you can ask Him to resolve a problem, and you can thank Him for what He's already done—and you can do it all day long.

Never wait for fitter time or place to talk to him.
To wait till you go to church or to your room
is to make him wait. He will listen as you walk.

GEORGE MACDONALD

YOUR DAILY REFLECTIONS

_____

_____

_____

_____

*I've decided that there's nothing better to do than go ahead
and have a good time and get the most we can out of life.*
ECCLESIASTES 3:9 THE MESSAGE

You've heard the expression, "That's just the way life is." It sounds like an injustice that has to be endured. Or you've heard, "Life is beautiful," and you wonder if the speaker ever held a nine-to-five job, paid bills, or took care of a house full of children. The truth is that life consists of all of these things and much more.

God has given you life, but He hasn't left you to navigate through all of its wonders, difficulties, hard work, and happiness on your own. He has also given you clear instructions on how to live that life. The Bible is your handbook. Follow its commandments and principles, and you'll get the most out of every day in this life and the next.

Life is far more than pleasures, possessions, or plaques on the wall. Life, in all its many facets, is a gift from God every day.

The value of life lies not in the length of days,
but in the use we make of them.
MICHEL DE MONTAIGNE

YOUR DAILY REFLECTIONS

_____

_____

_____

_____

Speak each man the truth to his neighbor.

ZECHARIAH 8:16

You know that telling the truth in a court of law is important. You solemnly promise that you will tell the truth, the whole truth, and nothing but the truth. You may even be asked to place your hand on a Bible to remind you of how serious your promise is.

But what about day-to-day life where you're not "under oath"? Many people feel it's acceptable to mislead others or outright lie in daily life. To them it's a matter of convenience to avoid confrontations and consequences. But that doesn't make it right.

God wants you to speak the truth to others. Do so and you'll have a reputation of being honest. Life will be simpler. Best of all, you'll have the satisfaction of knowing that you're living a life that honors God.

Honesty has a beautiful and refreshing simplicity about it. No ulterior motives. No hidden meanings.

CHARLES R. SWINDOLL

YOUR DAILY REFLECTIONS

_____

_____

_____

_____

All hard work brings a profit,
but mere talk leads only to poverty.

PROVERBS 14:23 NIV

Perseverance means keeping at something and refusing to quit until it's done. That isn't a problem when you're doing something you enjoy. Every hour that you work on your hobby—whether restoring a vintage auto or gardening—is a pleasure.

Where you need perseverance is when you're working on an unpleasant, long-term project. It requires self-discipline to diligently work at it every day without procrastinating.

How do you motivate yourself? Pray for God's inspiration; take breaks; track your progress; joke about it; play music; get help; think about how you'll spend the money or enjoy the reward it will yield. Remind yourself why you're doing it. And remember: this, too, shall pass.

Great works are performed, not by strength,
but by perseverance.

SAMUEL JOHNSON

YOUR DAILY REFLECTIONS

_____

_____

_____

_____

That which we have seen and heard we declare to you,
that you also may have fellowship with us;
and truly our fellowship is with the Father
and with His Son Jesus Christ.

1 JOHN 1:3

It's acceptable to refer to any gathering as "fellowship," but the Bible uses the term to denote a depth of sharing and communion that is far more rare than it should be.

True fellowship is essential, because there are things that God can do for you through the ministry of a body of believers that He seems to choose to do in no other way. Fellowship also provides the opportunity for you to exercise your spiritual gifts, something that cannot often be done outside an assembly of Christians.

Seek out the deep sharing and community that makes for true fellowship. It will draw you closer to your brothers and sisters—and to God.

We will win the world when we realize that fellowship,
not evangelism, must be our primary emphasis.

JESS MOODY

YOUR DAILY REFLECTIONS

_____

_____

_____

_____

God's angel sets up a circle of protection around us
while we pray.

PSALM 34:7 THE MESSAGE

Some people believe that everything happens for a reason. Others think that life simply happens and God's children are touched with pain and accidents like everyone else. Who's right? That's a question that may not be answered in this life.

What you can be sure of is that God has the power to protect you and He has promised to do so. When you pray, He can do the miraculous to keep you safe. And yet, bad things do happen to good people. It is best to remember that even when you find yourself passing through the valley of the shadow of death, God will be with you. He will walk every inch of that valley with you. And together you will reach the other side.

Those who walk in God's shadow
are not threatened by the storm.

ANDREA GARNEY

YOUR DAILY REFLECTIONS

_____

_____

_____

_____

*Jesus said, "It is your Father's good pleasure
to give you the kingdom."*

LUKE 12:32

God loved you enough to send Jesus to die on the cross for you and take away the sin that separated you from Him. Now you can look forward to eternal life in Heaven.

But God doesn't stop there. As Paul asked, "He who did not spare His own Son ... how shall He not with Him also freely give us all things?" (Romans 8:32). God loves you enough to not only give you an unbelievably wonderful future in Heaven, but to do loving things for you here and now.

God is not a stingy Father. He is lavish and generous with His love. If you've been missing out on the benefits of being His child, draw near to Him today.

God's love is always supernatural, always a miracle,
always the last thing we deserve.

ROBERT HORN

YOUR DAILY REFLECTIONS

_____

_____

_____

_____

Our only power and success comes from God.

2 CORINTHIANS 3:5 TLB

It is God's will for you to succeed both in your spiritual life and in your daily labors. If you excel in your work but neglect your soul, you may end up with every material blessing, but find that none of it satisfies. If you are deeply spiritual but unsuccessful and struggling in your work, you will be unable to properly provide for your family. God knows that both are important.

Success in one area of your life does not guarantee success in others, so always do your best and pray over every sphere of your life. God wants to bless you in every way. He wants you to succeed.

Three qualities vital to success: toil, solitude, prayer.

CARL SANDBERG

YOUR DAILY REFLECTIONS

_____

_____

_____

_____

I meditate on You in the night watches.

PSALM 63:6

When you need to take a break from the busy rush of life and recharge your batteries, nothing works like meditation—focusing your thoughts on God. Get quiet for a few moments and reflect on God's greatness, His love, and His tenderness. Imagine Him creating the earth and all that dwells in it. Think for a while about the greatness of God in your own life. What has He done for you?

It's also productive to reflect on God's character—perfectly good, perfectly just, perfectly wise. As you meditate on God and His attributes, you will begin to feel that you know Him better. You will gain new confidence to place yourself and your affairs in His care.

If we bring our minds back again and again to God,
we shall be gradually giving the central place to God,
not only in our inner selves,
but in our practical everyday lives.

PAUL TOURNIER

YOUR DAILY REFLECTIONS

_____

_____

_____

_____

Be faithful until death, and I will give you the crown of life.
REVELATION 2:10

Eugene Peterson says that faithfulness is "a long obedience in the same direction." What a wonderful insight. Faithfulness is a virtue that can only be proven over time. It's not about who's there at the beginning, but who is still there at the end. When others go, will you stay? When others quit, will you hang on? That's the crux of faithfulness.

God has promised to be with you through every circumstance of your life—good and bad. He promises never to leave you nor forsake you. He has pledged His faithfulness. Will you be faithful to Him? Will you choose to trust Him when times are tough? Let God know that He can count on you.

I do not pray for success; I ask for faithfulness.
MOTHER TERESA

YOUR DAILY REFLECTIONS

_____

_____

_____

_____

They shall dwell safely, and no one shall make them afraid.

EZEKIEL 34:28

Security is more than just locking up. Security also refers to anything you count on to provide for your family, such as putting savings in the bank or having a steady job, so you can pay your bills. There are practical steps you can take to make your life secure, and God requires you to take those steps.

Your ultimate security, however, is to have God looking out for you. That's why once you have done all you can, it is wise to pray and commit your security and well-being, and that of your family, into His hands.

God has not promised to protect you from every dip in the stock market or every downsizing in your workplace, but you are His child and He has promised that He will always provide for you. You can rest securely in His care.

The saints in heaven are happier but no more secure
than are true believers here in this world.

LORAINE BOETHNER

YOUR DAILY REFLECTIONS

_____

_____

_____

_____

*Jesus said, "Walk out into the fields
and look at the wildflowers."*
MATTHEW 6:28 THE MESSAGE

The Bible says that the heavens and the earth proclaim the glory of God. They serve as evidence of His power and majesty. They confirm that He is indeed great enough to handle your life—guiding you to the fulfillment of His plan for you and foiling any foe that might try to obstruct your path.

So look around you and see the glory of your God. Pause and consider the magnificence of a simple flower or the complexity of a common tree. Glance up at the sky and reflect on the fact that God has created an atmosphere capable of sustaining our lives. Look at His handiwork and you will say as He did, "It is good."

We can almost smell the aroma of God's beauty
in the fresh spring flowers.
His breath surrounds us in the warm summer breezes.
GALE HEIDE

YOUR DAILY REFLECTIONS

_____

_____

_____

_____

Who is this King of Glory?
The Lord, strong and mighty, invincible in battle.

PSALM 24:8 TLB

Talk about strength, God has real strength! You may work out at the gym every day and be in top physical form. You may be fit and healthy and physically strong—but God can move mountains. There are no limits to His strength.

So as you do your weight training, properly building up and improving your own physical strength, take advantage of the opportunity to remind yourself that God is stronger than you will ever be. He is strong enough to meet any need you might have—whether it's physical, emotional, or spiritual.

No matter how weak or strong you may be, you will always be strong enough to meet the challenge when God adds His muscle to yours.

When a man has no strength, if he leans on God,
he becomes powerful.

DWIGHT LYMAN MOODY

YOUR DAILY REFLECTIONS

_____

_____

_____

_____

*Jesus said, "These you ought to have done,
without leaving the others undone."*

MATTHEW 23:23 THE MESSAGE

Do you have a clear understanding of what is most important in life? Jesus said that it was more important to store treasure in Heaven than to seek earthly riches. He instructed His disciples to put the things of God even before their physical needs.

The good news is that once you know what to put at the top of your list, it's easier to decide what to do with the rest. Ask yourself, "Would God want me to put my work ahead of my family's needs? Is God pleased when I make money my first concern?"

God wants you to have a good life, filled with love, peace, and joy. When you let Him help you get your priorities in order, you can bet that's where you're headed.

When first things are put first,
second things are not suppressed but increased.

C. S. LEWIS

YOUR DAILY REFLECTIONS

_____

_____

_____

_____

The peace of God, which surpasses all understanding,
will guard your hearts and minds through Christ Jesus.

PHILIPPIANS 4:7

It's not hard to be relaxed and peaceful when everything is going smoothly and your problems are all under control. But that's not real peace. Real peace is the inner calm God's Spirit gives you even when the world around you is chaotic, stress is bearing down on you, and things are going right off the rails at work and at home.

You get that kind of peace by trusting God and keeping your heart focused on Him. In return, His peace will keep you calm and under control—better able to process solutions and deal effectively with circumstances. Don't settle for a fragile peace that can't handle all that life is handing you. Put your hand in God's hand.

Christ alone can bring lasting peace—
peace with God—peace among men and nations—
and peace within our hearts.

BILLY GRAHAM

YOUR DAILY REFLECTIONS

_____

_____

_____

_____

Celebrate God all day, every day. I mean, revel in him!
PHILIPPIANS 4:4 THE MESSAGE

God knows that some people are cheerful and expressive and others are more serious and quiet, yet He tells all Christians—including you—to rejoice! What's the deal?

Joy is not necessarily wild exuberance, but rather, a steady, enduring inner happiness. It is anchored in God, who is seated high above the circumstances of your life. As long as you are holding on to Him, you can be joyful, even in the midst of sadness and distress. King David was.

Even when his enemies were hunting him down and closing in, David was able to compose joyful psalms of praise to God. He rejoiced in his understanding that God, His Father, could flatten any army, resolve any conflict, and confuse the plans of those who sought to kill him. He was joyful in the Lord.

Joy is an unceasing fountain bubbling up in the heart;
a secret spring the world can't see
and doesn't know anything about.
DWIGHT LYMAN MOODY

YOUR DAILY REFLECTIONS

_____

_____

_____

_____

The fear of the LORD is the beginning of wisdom;
a good understanding have all those who do
His commandments. His praise endures forever.

PSALM 111:10

It's good to have knowledge, but just knowing facts and figures won't make you a better person. Knowing what to do with the information you have—wisdom—has the power to change your life and the lives of others.

People gain conventional wisdom as they go through life, primarily by learning from their mistakes. Godly wisdom, however, is a gift from God. Solomon, the biblical king known for his wisdom, received his insights a diffferent way: he simply asked.

You can ask for wisdom too. God knows that you will face confusing situations at times. But if you ask for it, He has promised to give you the wisdom you need—unless you'd rather learn things the hard way.

Wisdom is the application of knowledge.

AUTHOR UNKNOWN

YOUR DAILY REFLECTIONS

_____

_____

_____

_____

Jesus said, "Come off by yourselves;
let's take a break and get a little rest."

MARK 6:31 THE MESSAGE

Jesus knew what it was like to be busy. The Bible says that He ministered to the poor, the sick, and the spiritually needy from dawn to dusk. That's why He insisted on taking a breather. He knew that neither He nor His disciples could just keep up the pace without getting away for a rest. And He knows you need rest too.

So, when you feel yourself getting impatient and frayed around the edges, stop for a while. Let your mind and body catch up. God will bless your work even more when you get back to it. Many find that their creativity, problem-solving abilities, and coping skills all get a kick upward when they return after even a five- or ten-minute break.

Solitude is the soul's best friend.

CHARLES COTTON

YOUR DAILY REFLECTIONS

_____

_____

_____

_____

Jesus said, "If you abide in Me, and My words abide in you,
you will ask what you desire, and it shall be done for you."
JOHN 15:7

Aladdin rubbed his Arabian lamp and—Poof!—a genie appeared, granting whatever he wished. If you're expecting your prayer wishes to be fulfilled in the same way, you are bound to become frustrated.

Prayer has less to do with a wish list and more to do with your relationship with God. As you develop that relationship through prayer and abiding in God's Word, you begin to desire the things that God desires for you. And that's the key to effective prayer. Ask according to His will, and it will be done.

Prayer is not a vending machine that spits out
the appropriate reward.
It is a call to a loving God to relate to us.
PHILIP YANCY AND TIM STAFFORD

YOUR DAILY REFLECTIONS

_____

_____

_____

_____

May the God of hope fill you with all joy
and peace in believing, that you may abound
in hope by the power of the Holy Spirit.

ROMANS 15:13

Imagine for a moment how hopeless the followers of Jesus Christ must have felt as they wrapped His lifeless body in grave clothes and laid it in a borrowed tomb. Jesus had tried to tell them what was coming. He tried to make them understand that they would see Him again, that He would return to them, but they simply could not take hold.

Hope replaced despair, however, when they saw Jesus standing before them—risen from the dead. Christ's resurrection from the dead holds the key to your hope as well. Because He is alive, you have hope of life after death, hope of one day again seeing your loved ones who have died in the Lord, hope of spending eternity in a place where our loving God rules and reigns.

Hope can see heaven through the thickest clouds.

THOMAS BENTON BROOKS

YOUR DAILY REFLECTIONS

_____

_____

_____

_____

From that time Jesus began to preach and to say,
"Repent, for the kingdom of heaven is at hand."

MATTHEW 4:17

Simply stated, Heaven is this: to know the only true God—the Father and His Son, Jesus Christ, whom He has sent. After death, Christians will know the delight of God's full presence. That will be Heaven.

But did you know that you can feel the delight of God's presence right now, here on Earth? When you spend time with God in prayer, read the words He's written to you in the Bible, and spend time meditating on His greatness, you are experiencing a foretaste of what it will be like in your heavenly home. Remember it, relish it, close your eyes and let yourself be enveloped by God's loving presence. It is your future, your eternity.

Heaven is a prepared place for a prepared people.

LEWIS SPERRY CHAFER

YOUR DAILY REFLECTIONS

_____

_____

_____

_____

*Whatever happens, keep thanking God because
of Jesus Christ. This is what God wants you to do.*
1 THESSALONIANS 5:18 CEV

You don't need a turkey to celebrate thanksgiving. All you need is a reason. God has given you more reasons to be thankful than He's created stars in the sky. So, why wait?

Start with what you see—the clothes you're wearing, the food in the fridge, the beauty of a summer day. Then, think about the people you love and how they've touched your life. Next, consider what God's given you that can't be held in your hands—things like hope, forgiveness, and your future home in Heaven. Sit quietly as God brings even more reasons to mind.

Stopping to say "thanks" will remind you of how big God is and how good your life is when He's in it, no matter what day it is.

A humble mind is the soil out of which
thanks naturally grows.

HENRY WARD BEECHER

YOUR DAILY REFLECTIONS

_____

_____

_____

_____

*Jesus said, "You shall know the truth,
and the truth shall make you free."*

JOHN 8:32

The Bible says that fear can make you a captive—and truth can set you free. What truth is it that has this amazing power over fear? The truth that Jesus Christ has conquered sin, death, and the grave. He has mastered every situation that you could possibly face, forgiven every sin you could possibly commit, and given you eternal life.

So why would you choose to stay inside your prison cell? Take hold of the truth. Meditate on it until you see the doors swinging open before you. You are free to go, to live, to thrive, to love, to be loved, to be fulfilled as a person. And that's the truth!

I think the most important quality
in a person concerned with religion
is absolute devotion to truth.

ALBERT SCHWEITZER

YOUR DAILY REFLECTIONS

_____

_____

_____

_____

If you puff yourself up, you'll get the wind
knocked out of you. But if you're content to
simply be yourself, your life will count for plenty.

MATTHEW 23:11 THE MESSAGE

Many people associate humility with false modesty, denigrating themselves and talking down their accomplishments before others. That couldn't be further from the truth. Humility is really just the freedom to be yourself. It's a license to stop pretending.

God knows exactly who you are, and He likes you. He would never ask you to represent yourself as less than His marvelous creation. He wants you to be exactly who you are—no prideful extensions, no hokey denials. That's humility. When you learn to walk in humility, God is much freer to work in your life.

Human personality and individuality written
and signed by God on each human countenance . . .
is something altogether sacred, something for
the resurrection, for eternal life.

LÉON BLOY

YOUR DAILY REFLECTIONS

_____

_____

_____

_____

Do your best to present yourself to God as one approved,
a workman who does not need to be ashamed
and who correctly handles the word of truth.

2 TIMOTHY 2:15 NIV

Most people suffer from chronic performance anxiety. Is that the case with you? Are you constantly wondering what kind of reviews you will receive from your spouse, your children, you boss, your friends, your coworkers? If so, here's a little stage wisdom to help you cope.

Kill the foot lights and turn up the house lights. When you do, you will see that there is only one VIP in the audience—God. Ultimately, His review is the only one that matters. When you live your life in a manner that is pleasing to Him, it will build your confidence because it will be established on something solid, instead of on the shifting sands of people's opinions. So, chase away your anxiety and live your life for God. You're bound to be a hit with Him.

God is the only goal worthy of man's efforts.

SAINT AUGUSTINE OF HIPPO

YOUR DAILY REFLECTIONS

_____

_____

_____

_____

Forgetting those things which are behind and reaching forward
to those things which are ahead, I press toward the goal
for the prize of the upward call of God in Christ Jesus.

PHILIPPIANS 3:13–14

Ask any successful runner where he focuses his attention during a race, and he'll tell you he does not watch his competitors, his feet, or the crowd. Rather, his attention stays fixed on the finish line. He focuses on his goal—and that disciplined focus urges him onward till his race is completed.

If you desire to make the most of the life God has given you, you must be able to focus on your goal as well. Ask God to reveal His plan for your life. Ask Him to help you see the markers along the way. Then, lace up your running shoes and go for it. God will be with you throughout the race. And He will be there to present you with your prize when you cross the finish line.

The goal of a virtuous life is to become like God.

GREGORY OF NYSSA

YOUR DAILY REFLECTIONS

_____

_____

_____

_____

"Lord, help!" they cried, and he did!
He led them straight to safety.

PSALM 107:6–7 TLB

Imagine yourself standing on the edge of a field of land mines, wondering how you'll get across to safety. Suddenly, someone appears who tells you that he knows where all the mines are. "I can lead you through safely," he says.

How would you answer? Would you say, "No thanks. I don't need your help." Of course not. More likely, you would say, "Thanks. I'll follow and stay close."

God knows that life can be like a big field of land mines. He knows—and He wants to help you get to the other side safely. He will never impose His ways on you, but you would be wise to follow and stay close.

All the way my Savior leads me;
what have I to ask beside?
Can I doubt His tender mercy,
who through life has been my guide.

FRANCES JANE VAN ALSTYNE

YOUR DAILY REFLECTIONS

_____

_____

_____

_____

The LORD is gracious and full of compassion,
slow to anger and great in mercy.

PSALM 145:8

Do you find it difficult to feel compassion for certain people? A professional athlete gets suspended for punching out a referee. A neighbor wrecks his car after driving drunk. A teenager does poorly in school simply because he won't take the time to study. It must seem to you that they really don't deserve your compassion.

When you feel that way, it's good to remember that you were once in the same condition. You may not have punched a referee or driven drunk, but you almost certainly behaved foolishly in some way. And yet, God looked down on you and poured out His compassion on you when you least deserved it. Be the child of your Father in Heaven. Reach out to others—even if they don't deserve it.

It is a fair rule of thumb that only that love of neighbor,
which can also draw people to Christ is truly
a reflection of that love for God which is its source.

JEREMY C. JACKSON

YOUR DAILY REFLECTIONS

_____

_____

_____

_____

Jesus answered and said to them,
"Those who are well have no need of a physician,
but those who are sick. I have not come to call the righteous,
but sinners, to repentance."

LUKE 5:31

When Jesus and His disciples walked through the hill country of Nazareth, He ministered to all who came to Him. He touched those who needed healing and made them well. He healed those whose minds were sick and failing. But Jesus also spoke of those who needed spiritual healing—those whose souls were sick with sin and on the verge of spiritual death. Jesus brought healing to every part of His followers' lives.

Perhaps your body is fit and healthy, your mind quick and strong, but you have no relationship with God. Your spirit has been mortally wounded and only God can make you whole again. Seek Him out. Tell Him what you need. He's the Great Physician.

True repentance has a double aspect.
It looks upon things past with a weeping eye,
and upon the future with a watchful eye.

ROBERT SMITH

YOUR DAILY REFLECTIONS

_____

_____

_____

_____

Trust in the LORD with all your heart, and lean not
on your own understanding; in all your ways
acknowledge Him, and He shall direct your paths.

PROVERBS 3:5–6

People say they want to make their own decisions, set their own course. But being a decision maker can be tough. After all, the world is constantly changing. You may have a lead on the past and the present, but the future is anyone's guess.

Unless … you happen to know the One who knows the future. No—He isn't the great fortuneteller in the sky, but He will give you the wisdom you need to make good choices. He will show you timeless principles in the Bible and lead you to wise people who can help you put things into proper perspective. And when you've made the right decision, He'll fill your heart with His peace.

In making our decisions, we must use the brains
that God has given us. But we must also use
our hearts which He also gave us.

FULTON OURSLER

YOUR DAILY REFLECTIONS

_____

_____

_____

_____

He has made us accepted in the Beloved.

EPHESIANS 1:6

Many people search their entire lives for the acceptance of others. They strive to wear the right clothes, do the right things, speak the right words—all in an attempt to make others like them. Are you one of those people?

If so, you are searching for something you already have. God created you, and He accepts you just the way you are. There is nothing you can do or say or think that will make Him love you more than He already does.

It's all right to want others to like you—but you aren't likely to find what you really desire until you see yourself as God sees you.

Acceptance means you are valuable just as you are.
It allows you to be the real you.

GLADYS M. HUNT

YOUR DAILY REFLECTIONS

_____

_____

_____

_____

You have also given me the shield of your salvation;
Your right hand has held me up,
Your gentleness has made me great.

PSALM 18:35

The Bible speaks of Jesus Christ as the Lion of the Tribe of Judah. It's quite a daunting title—fierce and commanding. And yet, Jesus told His disciples that He is "gentle and humble in heart." Which description is true? Both.

You may think that gentleness equates to weakness. But that simply isn't so. Gentleness is actually controlled strength. It is the ability to choose to reach out to another person with tenderness and caring when it is within your power to crush and destroy.

Choose to be gentle with those God has placed in your life—your spouse, your children, your coworkers. In that way, you are following in the footsteps of Jesus.

When you encounter difficulties and contradictions,
do not try to break them,
but bend them with gentleness and time.

FRANCIS DE SALES

YOUR DAILY REFLECTIONS

_____

_____

_____

_____

Whoever calls on the name of the Lord shall be saved.

ACTS 2:21

Some people believe that you can't be certain of your salvation until after you die. But the New Testament is filled with assurances—that God's deep desire is for everyone to receive the gift of salvation, that Christ's sacrifice on the cross was sufficient to cover all sin, that any person who is forgiven and cleansed by Christ's blood is heir to eternal life.

God doesn't want you to live your life wondering if you will make it to Heaven. He wants you to know that He is preparing a place for you. Jesus said to the thief who hung beside Him on the cross, "This day you will be with me in paradise." That day, with his dying breath, a criminal turned to Jesus and received the assurance of his salvation.

The assurance of salvation is one
of God's beautiful gifts. Every believer ought to know
that he possesses salvation.

GEORGE SWEETING

YOUR DAILY REFLECTIONS

_____

_____

_____

_____

Blessed be the God and Father of our Lord Jesus Christ,
who has blessed us with every spiritual blessing
in the heavenly places in Christ.

EPHESIANS 1:3

Blessing is the currency of the Kingdom of God. When He created man and woman and set them on the earth, He blessed them with an abundance of cool clear water, fresh air, fertile soil. When men and women turn to God and open their hearts to Him, another layer of blessing is applied—eternal life, forgiveness of sin, the love of a caring heavenly Father. And that's not all!

There are also blessings that come as a result of obeying the principles in God's Word. The Bible says to obey God's commandments and you will be blessed. Share generously with the poor and you will be blessed, honor your father and mother and you will be blessed. Reach out to God. He wants to bless you!

Let never day nor night unhallow'd pass,
but still remember what the Lord hath done.

WILLIAM SHAKESPEARE

YOUR DAILY REFLECTIONS

_____

_____

_____

_____

Anyone who does what is good is from God.
                                        3 JOHN 1:11 NIV

Some people believe that being good will get them into Heaven. But being a "good" man or a "good" woman won't do it. To measure up to God's standard, you must be more than good; you must be perfect—and human beings just aren't capable of that.

That's why God sent His Son, Jesus Christ, to live a life of perfect goodness—a life completely pleasing to God—and then sacrifice that perfect life for you. Don't count on being good enough to spend eternity with God. You'll never make it. Instead, count on the goodness of Christ—God's perfect Son—to get you there.

God cannot accept goodness from me.
He can only accept my badness, and he will give me
the solid goodness of the Lord Jesus in exchange for it.
                                        OSWALD CHAMBERS

YOUR DAILY REFLECTIONS

_____

_____

_____

_____

Jesus said to Thomas, "Reach your finger here,
and look at My hands; and reach your hand here,
and put it into My side. Do not be unbelieving, but believing."
JOHN 20:27

Belief is not the absence of doubt, but the decision to stand in the midst of your doubts. Thomas had his doubts when the other disciples told him that Jesus had risen from the dead. But when Jesus appeared, He never condemned Thomas. Instead, He gave him evidence. He encouraged Thomas to touch Him and believe.

God doesn't condemn you for your doubts either. He just wants you to reach out to Him, to let Him prove to you that He does indeed exist. He desires to win you with His love and draw you with His kindness. Bring your doubts to Jesus; lay them at His feet in prayer. Let Him turn your doubts to belief.

More persons, on the whole, are humbugged
by believing in nothing, than by believing in too much.
P. T. BARNUM

YOUR DAILY REFLECTIONS

_____

_____

_____

_____

*Jesus said, "Let the little children come to Me,
and do not forbid them; for of such is the kingdom of heaven."*
MATTHEW 19:13–14

"Once a parent, always a parent," as the wise old saying goes. If you have children of any age, you know that they will always be in your heart. God never intended parenting to be an "until you're grown and out of the house" proposition. He meant it to last a lifetime. Yes, indeed, the relationship changes, but it never disappears.

God wants you to know that you will always be His child. As you grow and mature, there will be times of discipline, times of instruction, times of close parental care. And as you grow older, there will be times of blessed friendship and sweet communion with your Father God. Your relationship will change with time, but it will last for eternity.

Ideal parenting is modeled after
the relationship between God and man.
JAMES DOBSON

YOUR DAILY REFLECTIONS

_____

_____

_____

_____

*We all, with unveiled face, beholding as in a mirror
the glory of the Lord, are being transformed into the same
image from glory to glory, just as by the Spirit of God.*

2 CORINTHIANS 3:18

One of the most exciting things about having a relationship with God is that there is always more on the horizon. The life of a believer is a life of expectancy. A. B. Simpson was once asked if he believed in a "second blessing" experience after salvation. "Yes," he replied, "and a third and fourth! God always has more for you."

Just as He provided the children of Israel with fresh manna to eat each morning, God's mercies are new for you each morning as well. Don't dwell in the past. Wait expectantly for the manna God has for you today. You won't be disappointed.

Complacency is a deadly foe of all spiritual growth.
Acute desire must be present or there will be
no manifestation of Christ to His people.
He waits to be wanted.

A. W. TOZER

YOUR DAILY REFLECTIONS

_____

_____

_____

_____

Jesus said, "I am the resurrection and the life.
He who believes in Me, though he may die, he shall live.
And whoever lives and believes in Me shall never die."
JOHN 11:25–26

When you hear the phrase "eternal life," you probably think of Heaven, which is understandable. But you do not have to wait for Heaven; eternal life begins now, the moment you receive Christ as Savior. This means your life has a new dimension—an eternal, undying quality it never had before. From now on, everything is a prelude, a dress rehearsal for your heavenly future.

This perspective will change your priorities and purpose. Some activities will become less important in light of heavenly values. Deadlines, worries, and time restraints will not be oppressive to the person with a heavenly view. Spend your day with the conscious knowledge of eternal life, and see the difference it makes!

God has set the quality of everlastingness in our hearts.

A. W. TOZER

YOUR DAILY REFLECTIONS

_____

_____

_____

_____

Let your conduct be without covetousness, and be content
with such things as you have. For He Himself has said,
"I will never leave you nor forsake you."

HEBREWS 13:5

You may find contentment to be one of the more difficult Christian virtues to develop. Every day you are bombarded with advertising messages that, by and large, seek to make you discontent so that you can be persuaded to fill your new-found need with some new possession.

Think of it this way: Contentment is a by-product of thankfulness. Set aside some time each day to thank God for all He has done for you. And verbalize your thanks. Count your blessings, one by one, thanking God for each and every one. Soon you will have a new understanding of what you have, rather than what you don't have.

When we cannot find contentment in ourselves,
it is useless to seek it elsewhere.

FRANÇOIS LA ROCHEFOUCAULD

YOUR DAILY REFLECTIONS

_____

_____

_____

_____

*Let us consider one another in order to stir up love
and good works, not forsaking the assembling of ourselves
together, as is the manner of some, but exhorting one another,
and so much the more as you see the Day approaching.*

HEBREWS 10:25

You can't be a part of a church fellowship for very long without encountering friction. The church is made up of imperfect human beings just like you. God doesn't expect you to pretend it isn't so. Instead, He asks you to love and forgive and join hands.

If you are feeling frustrated by conflict in your church, pray for the grace to show love to your brothers and sisters in Christ. Ask God to bring unity beginning with your own heart. One day, in Heaven, God's Church—those whom He has redeemed—will be united and flawless in every way. But for now, God asks you to be kind, humble, loving, and forgiving.

A church is a hospital for sinners,
not a museum for saints.

L. L. NASH

YOUR DAILY REFLECTIONS

_____

_____

_____

_____

If we are faithless, He remains faithful;
He cannot deny Himself.

2 TIMOTHY 2:13

God's faithfulness grows out of the unchanging perfection of His nature. Because He is infinite and perfect in His love, mercy, and kindness, you can trust Him to be perfectly faithful in His care for you. Your friends may fail you; your own heart may fail you, but God never will. Divine faithfulness is just God being what He has always been and always will be.

That is why it is foolishness to think for a moment that God's faithfulness to you is in any way dependent upon your performance. Even if you have been faithless, turn your heart to the One who is ever faithful. He is always ready to take you in.

Upon God's faithfulness rests our whole hope
of future blessedness.

A. W. TOZER

YOUR DAILY REFLECTIONS

_____

_____

_____

_____

What is desired in a man is kindness.

PROVERBS 19:22

Y ou may think of benevolence only in terms of giving money, but there is much more to it than that. Benevolence is simply showing kindness; and in many cases, it is more a matter of opening your heart than your wallet.

In an age of hardness and cruelty, practicing benevolence is more difficult, but also more crucial. So many people are suffering for lack of a helping hand. Give to others with the same open-handed freedom that God has given to you. Do it out of your love for Him and in a spirit of thankfulness for what you have received from Him. He will bless you for it many times over.

The heart benevolent and kind the most resembles God.

ROBERT BURNS

YOUR DAILY REFLECTIONS

_____

_____

_____

_____

In Him we have redemption through His blood,
the forgiveness of sins, according to the riches of His grace.
EPHESIANS 1:7

Would you develop a relationship with someone who could bring nothing to the relationship? If it was all give and no take, would you even bother?

Now consider the fact that God's relationship with you is just that way. He created everything—there is nothing that you can give Him that He does not already have. That's what grace is all about. It is unmerited favor. God gives to you what you do not deserve, knowing full well that you can never pay Him back. All that you have is from His hand, through His matchless, infinite grace.

Will you be God's hand of grace extended to others?

Grace means the free, unmerited, unexpected love
of God, and all the benefits, delights, and comforts,
which flow from it. It means that while we were sinners
and enemies we have been treated as sons and heirs.
R .P. C. HANSON

YOUR DAILY REFLECTIONS

_____

_____

_____

_____

A friend loves at all times, and a brother is born for adversity.
PROVERBS 17:17

You may have heard of the counseling theory that suggests you limit your friendships to "safe" people—those with no emotional baggage that could drag you down. That doesn't sound right, does it? Not only could this severely limit your pool of potential friends, but it seems to violate the selfless example of Christ, who specialized in making friends of those who were down and out.

You could be a great influence for good in a needy person's life, simply by making friends with them. Certainly some people can be emotionally draining, and you should always ask God for wisdom when approaching a new relationship. He will always steer you in the right direction. And He will often point you to diamonds in the rough.

A real friend is one who walks in
when the rest of the world walks out.
WALTER WINCHELL

YOUR DAILY REFLECTIONS

_____

_____

_____

_____

*Since future victory is sure, be strong and steady, always
abounding in the Lord's work.*

1 CORINTHIANS 15:58 TLB

There are two ways of looking at the future. You can worry yourself silly, or you can place your future in the hands of God and walk forward with confidence and courage. It isn't that God wants you to be unconcerned about the future. Jesus urged His disciples to plan and prepare for what was ahead of them. But He also told them not to be consumed with worry.

God has a wonderful plan for your life—whether you are fifteen or fifty-five. He wants you to fearlessly face each day with your hand in His. Don't allow what might happen to rob you of your sense of excitement and anticipation. Go forward into the future with God.

I've read the last page of the Bible.
It's all going to turn out all right.

BILLY GRAHAM

YOUR DAILY REFLECTIONS

_____

_____

_____

_____

Blessed be the God and Father of our Lord Jesus Christ,
the Father of mercies and God of all comfort,
who comforts us in all our tribulation, that we may be able to
comfort those who are in any trouble, with the comfort
with which we ourselves are comforted by God.

2 CORINTHIANS 1:3–4

When you are going through tough times, you may wonder why God allows it. Only God knows the reasons. What you can be sure of is that He will be there for you, no matter what circumstance you encounter. His love and comfort are resources that will see you through your trial.

And don't forget that others are watching as you lean on God's comforting arm in the face of heartache and disappointment. Your example may show them where to turn when they encounter difficulties in their own lives. Your sorrow will not be in vain if you are able to lead one other person to the comforting arms of the Good Shepherd.

God does not comfort us to make us comfortable
but to make us comforters.

JOHN HENRY JOWETT

YOUR DAILY REFLECTIONS

_____

_____

_____

_____

> *They gave in a way we did not expect:*
> *They first gave themselves to the Lord and to us.*
> *This is what God wants.*
>
> 2 CORINTHIANS 8:5 NCV

The call to be generous can be frustrating for many people. "It's easy to be generous when you have lots of money." but you may say, "I'm struggling just to make ends meet."

The apostle Paul reveals the secret to Christian generosity. He says of the Macedonian churches, "They first gave themselves to the Lord and to us." True generosity is knowing your strengths and being willing to share them. It is giving of yourself—your time, talents, energy—rather than just your money. Give your heart to those in need. Then giving your money will be guided by the spirit of generosity.

> For the Macedonian Christians, giving was not a chore
> but a challenge, not a burden but a blessing.
> Giving was not something to be avoided,
> but a privilege to be desired.
>
> GEORGE SWEETING

YOUR DAILY REFLECTIONS

_____

_____

_____

_____

If You, Lord, should mark iniquities,
O Lord, who could stand? But there is forgiveness with You,
that You may be feared.

PSALM 130:3–4

God's forgiveness is so great that some preachers seem hesitant to speak of its fullness and immensity, for fear that people might sin more freely! It doesn't work that way, however. Jesus said that the one who is forgiven much loves much, and if you love God, you will want to obey Him.

You may feel that there are things you have done that could not possibly be forgiven. But you would be wrong about that. Christ died to pay for your sins, and His was the perfect sacrifice—the debt of sin paid once and forever. There is nothing you could have done that would be so terrible that His sacrifice will not cover it. Turn your heart to the Lord, and discover the boundless forgiveness of God.

There is only one person God cannot forgive—
the person who refuses to come to him for forgiveness.

AUTHOR UNKNOWN

YOUR DAILY REFLECTIONS

_____

_____

_____

_____

Many proclaim themselves loyal,
but who can find one worthy of trust?

PROVERBS 20:6 NRSV

Commitment is the key to the Christian life. No believer can have joy and peace until he has surrendered all to Jesus Christ.

Are you fully committed? You can find out by asking yourself a few questions: If God asked me to give up my greatest pleasure, would I do it? If He asked me to face my greatest fear, would I do it? If He asked me to do something embarrassing, costly, or difficult, would I do it?

If you can answer "yes" to these questions, you need not worry about your commitment. If you cannot answer "yes," pray that God will change your heart—and expect Him to test your decision.

Take my life, and let it be consecrated, Lord, to thee.

FRANCES RIDLEY HAVERGAL

YOUR DAILY REFLECTIONS

_____

_____

_____

_____

You are good, and do good; teach me Your statutes.

PSALM 119:68

The word "goodness" may conjure up an image in your mind of a Goody Two-shoes—the kind of person who never appears to do anything wrong and looks down his nose at the smallest failure in others. But true goodness has no trace of self-righteousness. It is, in fact, an attribute of God—one that, as His child, you can share.

Goodness is what motivates God to be so kind and caring to undeserving sinners. It is why He is so kind and gracious in answering our prayers. It is why He looks upon us with favor and blesses us with good things. How can you follow His example and practice goodness to others?

Goodness is love in action, love with its hand to
the plow, love with the burden on its back,
love following his footsteps
who went about continually doing good.

JAMES HAMILTON

YOUR DAILY REFLECTIONS

_____

_____

_____

_____

*There must be a spiritual renewal
of your thoughts and attitudes.*

EPHESIANS 4:23 NLT

When you become a child of God, you are given a fresh start—your sins are forgiven, your mistakes are behind you, and you have eternity ahead of you. Don't ever let go of that sense of newness.

The apostle Paul said that when you are in Christ, you are a new creation—that's present tense! Christ's life in you is perpetually new. And that's backed up by the prophet Jeremiah who said that God's mercies are new every morning. Never again allow your life to become stale and commonplace. Just as you wouldn't think of leaving the house in the morning without taking a shower, don't leave home without confessing your faults to God and walking away spiritually cleansed and refreshed.

The sense of newness is simply delicious.
It makes new the Bible, and friends, and all mankind,
and love, and spiritual things, and Sunday, and church,
and God Himself. So I've found.

TEMPLE GARDNER OF CAIRO

YOUR DAILY REFLECTIONS

_____

_____

_____

_____

*The angel said to her, "Do not be afraid, Mary, you have
found favor with God. You will be with child and give birth
to a son, and you are to give him the name Jesus.
He will be great and will be called the Son of the Most High."*

LUKE 1:30–32 NIV

You know the story—an infant, born in a stable,
worshiped by lowly shepherds and travelers from
the East. Sweet story. But does it hold any meaning for your
life today?

Consider this. The entire Bible pivots on this single
event in history. The Old Testament predicts it and the
New Testament confirms it. The child lying in that tiny
manger was no ordinary child—He was God incarnate,
come to live and die for you. The story won't be fully told
until you bow your knee to Bethlehem's Babe and call Him
the Lord of your life. If you have not already done so, make
Jesus your Lord today.

Christmas began in the heart of God.
It is complete only when it reaches the heart of man.

AUTHOR UNKNOWN

YOUR DAILY REFLECTIONS

_____

_____

_____

_____

To this end I also labor, striving according to
His working which works in me mightily.

COLOSSIANS 1:29

Have you ever wondered if life is worth the trouble? After all, it seems to be filled with heartache and disappointment and frustration. Sometimes, it's just plain boring and exhausting. God understands that you will sometimes feel like giving up. But He wants you to keep on going, refusing to quit until you have fulfilled the purpose for which He created you. That is determination.

God knows that every day of your life is important and worth living. One day there will be sweet rest. But for now, God is urging you to set your course and be determined to see it through. And you should know that He is even more determined than you could ever be to see you finish the race He's set before you.

I will go anywhere, provided it will be forward.

DAVID LIVINGSTONE

YOUR DAILY REFLECTIONS

_____

_____

_____

_____

Jesus said, "If you forgive men their trespasses,
your heavenly Father will also forgive you.
But if you do not forgive men their trespasses,
neither will your Father forgive your trespasses."

MATTHEW 6:14–15

Someone has wronged you. It's happened before, and you have no reason to believe that it won't happen again. Even though that person has asked for forgiveness, you wonder if he or she really deserves it.

The apostle Peter posed that very dilemma to Jesus one day. "Should I forgive as many as seven times?" he asked. Jesus' response must have startled him. "Not seven times," Jesus told him, "but seven times seventy."

God doesn't ask you to continue to place yourself in the path of another's hurtful acts. But He does instruct you to forgive after the fact—primarily for your own sake. Unforgiveness can only harm the one who holds it.

A cartoon in the New Yorker magazine showed an
exasperated father saying to his prodigal son,
"This is the fourth time we've killed the fatted calf."
God does that over and over in our lifetime.

BRUCE LARSON

YOUR DAILY REFLECTIONS

_____

_____

_____

_____

We should no longer be children …
but, speaking the truth in love, may grow up in all things
into Him who is the head—Christ.

EPHESIANS 4:14–15

Where there is life, there is growth. That fact certainly holds true in the physical realm. Children grow up. Trees grow tall. And in the same way, that fact applies to a life of faith. When you surrender yourself to God and become His child, a spiritual birth occurs, and a spiritual baby is born. From that day forward, spiritual growth begins to take place.

If you are a new babe in the life of faith, you can ensure your spiritual growth by finding nourishment in the Word of God, by learning from more mature believers, and by staying close to your heavenly Father. You have chosen to become a child of God. Now, let Him help you grow strong in the life of faith.

The strongest principle of growth lies in human choice.

GEORGE ELIOT

YOUR DAILY REFLECTIONS

_____

_____

_____

_____

*Jesus said, "Seek the kingdom of God,
and these things shall be added to you."*

LUKE 12:31

Jesus talked a lot about finances. Even then, people seemed preoccupied with money and possessions. He often reminded His disciples that gold and silver are the currencies of this world, but they cannot buy the most important things of all—love, peace, joy, hope, courage, understanding, happiness, wisdom, and eternal life. And that's the short list.

The truth is that money is really very limited. If you have trouble believing that, look at the lives of this world's wealthy. Their money cannot buy them loving relationships, stable lifestyles, or happy homes. Only God can provide those things.

Think long and hard before you invest your time and energy in the pursuit of money. Instead consider investing in the Kingdom of God.

A man's treatment of money is the most decisive test
of his character—how he makes it and how he spends it.

JAMES MOFFATT

YOUR DAILY REFLECTIONS

_____

_____

_____

_____

The Lord, He is the One who goes before you.
He will be with you, He will not leave you nor forsake you;
do not fear nor be dismayed.

Deuteronomy 31:8

Confidence is a positive attitude toward the future, an assurance that whatever tomorrow brings, you can meet its challenges. With that in mind, Christians should be the most confident people in the world. As a believer, you have the privilege of serving the God who holds the future in His hands.

Not one thing that happens to you surprises God or catches Him off guard. And He has promised to see you through every trial, every hardship, every heartbreak, every disappointment. Therefore, you can step into the future with confidence, knowing that the God who knows all and sees all has already paved the way before you and will be at your side until your journey's end.

Confidence in the natural world is self-reliance,
in the spiritual world it is God-reliance.

Oswald Chambers

YOUR DAILY REFLECTIONS

_____

_____

_____

_____

Comfort each other and edify one another,
just as you also are doing.

1 THESSALONIANS 5:11

The root of the word "encouragement" means to "put courage into." What a beautiful picture of one person standing beside another saying, "Take courage!" God has given you the ability to be that person to others. Ask Him to show you those who could use a kind word, an uplifting thought, a simple prayer. They could be strangers on the street or members of your own family.

Your encouragement may help someone walk when he or she might have stumbled. You might help someone stand firm instead of giving in. And encouraging others has yet another benefit—those around you are strengthened so that they can offer you an encouraging word when you need one.

I think many Christians are "dying on the vine"
for lack of encouragement from other believers.

CHARLES R. SWINDOLL

YOUR DAILY REFLECTIONS

_____

_____

_____

_____

Reflections
FOR THE
YEAR GONE-BY

REFLECTIONS FOR THE YEAR GONE-BY

REFLECTIONS FOR THE YEAR GONE-BY

REFLECTIONS FOR THE YEAR GONE-BY

REFLECTIONS FOR THE YEAR GONE-BY

REFLECTIONS FOR THE YEAR GONE-BY

Reflections
FOR THE
YEAR TO COME

REFLECTIONS FOR THE YEAR TO COME

REFLECTIONS FOR THE YEAR TO COME

REFLECTIONS FOR THE YEAR TO COME

REFLECTIONS FOR THE YEAR TO COME

REFERENCES

Scripture quotations marked KJV are taken from the King James Version of the Bible.

Scripture quotations marked NCV are taken from the International Children's Bible®, New Century Version®. Copyright © 1986, 1988, 1999 by Tommy Nelson™, a division of Thomas Nelson, Inc., Nashville, Tennessee 37214. Used by permission.

Scripture quotations marked THE MESSAGE are taken from The Message. Copyright © by Eugene H. Peterson, 1993, 1994, 1995, 1996. Used by permission of NavPress Publishing Group.

Scripture quotations marked NRSV are taken from The New Revised Standard Version Bible. Copyright © 1989 by the Division of Christian Education of the National Council of the Churches of Christ in the United States of America and are used by permission. All rights reserved.

Scripture quotations marked CEV are taken from The Contemporary English Version. Copyright © 1995 by the American Bible Society. Used by permission.

Scripture quotations marked NASB are taken from the New American Standard Bible®. Copyright © 1960, 1962, 1963, 1968, 1971, 1972, 1973, 1975, 1977, 1995 by The Lockman Foundation. Used by permission.

Scripture quotations marked TLB are taken from The Holy Bible, The Living Bible Translation. Copyright © 1971. Used by permission of Tyndale House Publishers, Incorporated, Wheaton, Illinois 60189. All rights reserved.

Scripture quotations marked NLT are taken from The Holy Bible, New Living Translation. Copyright © 1996. Used by permission of Tyndale House Publishers, Incorporated, Wheaton, Illinois 60189. All rights reserved.